MERCHANT
TAYLORS'
SCHOOLS

# MERCHANT TAYLORS' GIRLS' SCHOOL

Ex Libris

CONCORDIA PARVE RES CRESCUNT

**living with**
# ceramics

RIZZOLI
NEW YORK

# living with
# ceramics

**Annabel Freyberg**

*'The very 'marks' on the bottom of a piece of rare crockery are able to throw me into a gibbering ecstasy;*

*and I could forsake drowning relative to help dispute*

*about whether the stopple of a departed Buon Retiro scent bottle was genuine or spurious.'*

Mark Twain, 'A Tramp Abroad' (1880)

## PICTURE CREDITS

KEY: IA = THE INTERIOR ARCHIVE; CSS = CHRISTOPHER SIMON SYKES ;AW = ANDREW WOOD;
PR/II = PAUL RYAN/INTERNATIONAL INTERIORS; BRIDGEMAN ART LIBRARY = BAL; CHRISTIE'S IMAGES = CI

1 Ivan Terestchenko; 2-3 PR/II/architect Lee Mindel; 5 left BAL; 5 right CI; 6, 7 The Stapleton Collecton; 8 The National Trust; 9 National Portrait Gallery; 10 Angelo Hornak/Courtesy of the V & A; 11 Roderick Jellicoe/Stockspring Antiques; 12-13 IA/CSS; 14 Gary Atkins; 15 BAL/Sotheby's London; 16 Elizabeth Whiting & Associates/Brian Harrison; 17 Angelo Hornak; 18 Gerhard Trumler; 19 AKG London/Erich Lessing; 20-21 Ingalill Snitt; 20 Inside/Jacques Dirand; 23 Deidi von Schaewen/Lillian Williams; 24 IA/CSS; 25 PR/II/Axel Vervoordt; 26 above IA/Fritz von der Schulenburg; 26 below IA/CSS; 27 John Hall; 28 Gary Atkins; 29 Christian Sarramon; 30 IA/CSS; 31 IA/Tim Beddow; 32 & 33 Roderick Jellicoe/Stockspring Antiques; 34 above IA/Fritz von der Schulenburg; 34 below Arcaid/Jeremy Cockayne; 34-35 CI; 36 John Hall; 38-39 IA/Fritz von der Schulenburg; 40 above and below Robert Dawson; 41 Inside/Thibault Jeanson; 42 Stockspring Antiques; 43 above Mark Fiennes; 43 below CI; 44-45 Debbie Patterson/Glorious Interiors, Ebury Press; 46 BAL; 47 above Angelo Hornak; 47 centre & below CI; 48 Robert Harding Picture Library/Jan Baldwin/© IPC Magazines/Homes & Gardens; 48-49 IA/CSS; 50 & 51 above Roderick Jellicoe/Stockspring Antiques; 51 below Jonathan Horne; 52 Robert Harding Picture Library/Jonathan Pilkington/© IPC Magazines/Homes & Gardens; 53 Inside/Dominique Vorillon/B. Avnet; 54 BAL/City of Edinburgh Museums & Art Galleries, Scotland; 55 CI; 56-57 above & below John Hall; 57 above Arcaid/Rodney Weidland/Belle; 57 below Abode/Ian Parry; 58 above BAL/ Courtesy of the V & A; 58 below CI; 59 Jean-Pierre Godeaut/Monye Einstein; 60 above left Inside/Cote Ouest/Nicolas Millet/stylist M. Duveau; 60 above right Andreas von Einsiedel; 60 below IA/Tim Beddow; 61 IA/CSS; 62 Peter Chatterton; 63 Mrs Monro Ltd/ 65 IA/AW; 66-67 PR/II/Lee Mindel; 68 Ingalill Snitt; 69 Oberto Gili/Courtesy of House & Gardens/© The Condé Nast Publications, Inc.; 70 Stockspring; 71 CI; 72 & 73 IA/CSS; 74 Christian Sarramon; 74-75 PR/II/Joe Nahem; 76 above Andreas von Einsiedel; 76 below Robert Harding Picture Library/James Merrell/© IPC Magazines/Country Homes & Interiors; 77 IA/AW; 79 Annabel Freyberg/Stephen Long; 80-81 IA/AW; 82 Angelo Hornak/Annabel Freyberg; 83 World of Interiors/James Mortimer; 84 CI; 85 IA/James Mortimer; 86 Agence Top/Pascal Chevallier/made by Diego Giacometti/Hubert Givenchy; 88-89 IA/Fritz von der Schulenburg; 89 Scott Frances/ESTO/ Burr & McCallum; 90 IA/CSS; 91 Marie Claire Maison/Gilles de Chabaneix/Daniel Rozensztroch; 92-93 PR/II/Kriistina Ratia; 94-95, 96-97 IA/CSS; 97 Juliana Balint, J.B. Visual Press/Paul Ryan; 98 Jonathan Horne Antiques; 99 above Mary Wondrausch; 99 below BAL/Courtesy of the V & A; 100 Angelo Hornak; 100-101 IA/CSS; 102-103 Robert Harding Picture Library/© Brad Simmons Photography; 103 PR/II/Kriistina Ratia; 104 Private Collection/Adrian Sassoon; 105 Ianthe Ruthven/Deerfield, Massachusetts; 106 BAL/American Museum in Bath; 107 Bonhams; 108-109 all pictures Kosei Miya; 110 Inside/Jean-Paul Godeaut/stylist C. O'Byrne; 110-111 Inside/Guy Bouchet; 111 Ingalill Snitt; 112-113 Juliana Balint, J.B. Visual Press/Paul Ryan; 113 IA/Herbert Ypma; 114 BAL; 115 Narratives/Jan Baldwin; 116 The National Trust Photographic Library/Angelo Hornak; 117 Winterthur Museum; 118 BAL/CI; 119 Francesco Venturi/KEA; 120-121 Elizabeth Whiting & Associates/Neil Lorimer; 121 The National Trust; 122 Inside/Ivan Terestchenko; 123 Robert Harding Picture Library/Andreas von Einsiedel/© IPC Magazines/Country Homes & Interiors; 124 IA/CSS; 125 Ianthe Ruthven /Deerfield,Massachusetts; 126-27 IA/CSS; 128 Carolyn Stoddart-Scott; 129 IA/CSS; 130 Francesco Venturi/KEA; 131 above Guy Bouchet; 131 below Carolyn Stoddart-Scott/IA/CSS; 132-133 IA/Fritz von der Schulenburg; 133 above Andreas von Einsiedel; 133 centre Inside/Jacques Dirand; 133 below Ianthe Ruthven; 135 Elizabeth Whiting & Associates/Neil Lorimer; 136-137 IA/CSS; 138 Richard Dennis Gallery; 139 above BAL/Brighton Museum & Art Gallery; 139 below CI; 140 BAL; 141 CI; 142-143 IA/CSS; 144 BAL/Courtesy of the V & A; 145 CI; 146 above & below, 147 IA/CSS; 148 above Arcaid/Lucinda Lambton; 148 below IA/Cecilia Innes; 148-149 Arcaid/Lucinda Lambton; 150 CI; 151 IA/AW; 152 BAL/Fine Art Society, London; 153 CI; 154 above & below, 155, 156 IA/CSS; 157 CI; 158-159 IA/CSS; 160, 161 CI; 162 Stapleton Collection; 163 IA/Cecilia Innes; 164 IA/AW; 165 left York City Art Gallery; 165 right CI; 166, 167 IA/CSS; 168 Stapleton Collection; 169 Philip de Bay; 170 above PR/II/Jan des Bouvrie; 170 below PR/II/James Gager; 170-171 IA/AW; 171 above Agence Top/Nicolas Millet/designer Paul Mathieu & Michael Ray; 171 below left Narratives/Jan Baldwin; 171 below right IA/CSS; 172 BAL/Dreweatt Neate; 173 above left Christie's South Kensington; 173 centre left BAL/Laing Art Gallery, Newcastle-upon-Tyne, Tyne & Wear; 173 below right Angelo Hornak; 174 above & below, 175 IA/CSS; 176 Richard Dennis; 177 CI; 178 above James Mortimer; 178 centre Agence Top/Roland Beaufre/designer Tino Zervudachi; 178 below IA/AW; 179 IA/James Mortimer; 180 Target Gallery/Roy Fox; 181 above Richard Dennis/Philip de Bay; 181 below Target Gallery/Roy Fox; 182 James Mortimer; 182-183 IA/CSS; 184 Thea Burger Associates Inc.; 185 New Century Antiques; 186 above IA/James Mortimer; 186 below IA/AW; 187 above IA/James Mortimer; 187 below IA/AW; 188 CI; 189 Adrian Sassoon; 190-191, 191 above & below IA/James Mortimer; 192 IA/CSS; 194 above Agence Top/Pascal Hinous; 194 below, 195 IA/CSS; 196-197 Agence Top/Pascal Hinous; 198 Inside/Jean-Pierre Godeaut; 199 left Deidi von Schaewen; 199 IA/CSS; 200, 200-201 IA/Tim Beddow; 202 above Inside/Gilles de Chabaneix; 203 IA/CSS; 204, 204-205 IA/AW; 206 left Jean-Pierre Godeaut; 206 right IA/CSS; 207 Inside/Ivan Terestchenko; 208-209, 209 above & below, 210 above & below, 211 IA/AW; 212 Deidi von Schaewen/ Philippe Torreliat; 213 Marie Claire Maison/Nicolas Tosi/Catherine Ardouin; 214 & endpapers Angelo Hornak.

First published in the United States of America in 1999 by

RIZZOLI INTERNATIONAL PUBLICATIONS, INC.
300 Park Avenue South, New York, NY 10010

First published in Great Britain in 1999 by Laurence King Publishing

Text copyright © 1999 Annabel Freyberg

ISBN 0-8478-2201-X

LC 99-74819

Designed and typeset by Price Watkins

Printed in China

*half-title:* a pyramid of pears rises from an oriental blue-and-white bowl.
*title page:* a parade of early nineteenth-century basaltware.
*right:* a camel-backed vase designed by Christopher Dresser for Linthorpe Pottery.
*far right:* a lead-glazed earthenware dish by Bernard Palissy, c. 1550.

# contents

# introduction

**the joy of ceramics, their collection and display**

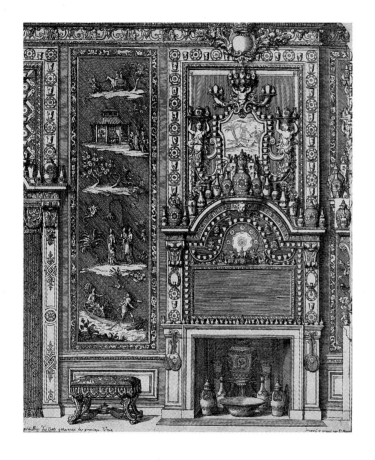

Ceramics have a heady allure. Ranging from crude brown vessels to the most delicate shimmering porcelain, they encompass superb sculpture, exquisite painting and rich luscious glazes. Their history stretches back thousands of years, they can be found in every country under the sun, and their form and decoration are a fascinating reflection of the era and society that produced them. Though all ceramics are fragile and easily shattered, millions of pieces survive, ready to be enjoyed by discriminating new admirers.

One of the most thrilling aspects of collecting ceramics is the sheer quantity of attractive varieties to choose from. Naturally some are exorbitantly priced, but many of the most desirable are still affordable. Indeed, whatever your budget there are numerous collecting options. In the past, collectors have tended to plump for a single subject: objects made by a particular factory; decorated by a specific painter; lustreware or coffee-cans. This book looks at looser but equally appealing collecting categories, focusing on ceramics that work well in a domestic setting. Pieces are shown in isolation and in people's homes, where shape, colour and style are often as important as rarity or value. The odd chip – rendering an object up to five times cheaper than a perfect one – is of infinitely less consequence than decorative value.

Many books on china concentrate on the specialist – and unaffordable – end of the market, neglecting the reasonably priced pieces more commonly encountered. This book aims to give a brief history of china's evolution in the West – where it has been a thrillingly experimental material since the seventeenth century – but also to include the pretty workaday ceramics that have developed in the wake of the most sophisticated: for example, Wemyss-ware jam pots alongside examples of Meissen *Deutsche Blumen*. Specific prices are not given because so much depends on an individual piece: its rarity, condition, date, attractiveness, local interest and other factors, which make cost vary enormously.

A ceramic artefact can be both beautiful and practical – why eat off dull china when a handsome piece is affordable, fun and just as hardy? It is marvellously portable too. Unlike a picture or a piece of furniture a pot can be moved around at will to create a new look. Like abstract painting, it can be mysterious, austere, soothing or plain pretty. It can be viewed on its own, or as an ingredient in a still life. Moreover, even in a modern context there is room for the antique: something eighteenth century can be unfamiliar, handsome and cost no more than a conical Clarice Cliff sugar shaker. While few antique pieces are without some signs of wear (though those that survive tend to be the best quality), their high-fired colours remain as bold as when first applied. Thus the hue of a tea service used by Jane Austen, or a Tang horse, is much the same as it was originally.

To add fuel to the collector's fire, almost every house is a repository of china, while shops, car boot sales and auctions offer temptation galore. There is enormous fun to be had from looking at and learning about different ceramics, whether the floral variety in your local tandoori or 'rustic' pottery encountered on holiday. What tradition do they fit into? What similar kinds should you look out for? And how can you display your finds to best effect? The following pages offer some suggestions.

The history of ceramics in the West is littered with obsessive collectors, among them the dandy Beau Brummell, a keen fan of Sèvres; William Gladstone, who was partial to Wedgwood; and Augustus the Strong, Elector of Saxony, and Meissen's founder, who once exchanged a regiment of dragoons for 48 Chinese vases. The earliest connoisseurs, in China, kept their finest pieces in silk-lined boxes, gazing at them only occasionally; in Europe, from the arrival of oriental porcelain at the end of the seventeenth century, collectors thrilled to the effect of massing it together. The greatest collector in England was Queen Mary II. Her taste was much copied, as the

above: Lady Betty Germain's china closet at Knole in Kent, photographed in 1900. A friend of the Sackvilles – and also of Horace Walpole, another china devotee – Lady Betty lived at Knole in the mid-eighteenth century and found a home there for her porcelain collection; the closet and some of the porcelain remain to this day. *right:* William Morris's restrained double shelves of china above the fireplace of the long drawing room at Kelmscott House in Hammersmith, London, where he lived from 1874 to 1896. The photograph was taken by Emery Walker in the 1890s. The fireplace tiles are Morris & Co, while among the rhythmically arranged plates are Iznik lustreware of the kind that influenced William De Morgan, who was himself encouraged to take up pottery by William Morris.

historian Lord Macaulay lamented two centuries later: 'Even statesmen and generals were not ashamed to be renowned as judges of teapots and dragons'.

Georgian taste was far more restrained than Stuart, though even in the mid-eighteenth century Chinese jars and vases continued to be displayed on or below pieces of furniture and as summer still lifes in fire-places. Figures moved from the dessert table to brackets; giant vases were often used as furnishings. By now, porcelain collecting was largely a feminine preserve. The Duchesses of Portland, Manchester, Norfolk and Somerset, and the Countess of Devonshire were noted devotees, while Lady Betty Germain's china room survives at Knole.

By then the quantity and range of ceramics available had increased to such an extent that the Dutch East India Co imported more in the five years between 1729 and 1734 than in the 80 years between 1602 and 1682. In addition European and English manu-factories were turning out fashionable and desirable wares, while visiting salerooms became fashionable from the mid-eighteenth century onwards. Possessors of special china closets included the noted connoisseur Horace Walpole. His closet at Strawberry Hill measured 4m by 2.9m (12ft by 9ft 9in); he lined it with gothicised shelves above its 'medieval wall tomb' of a mantelpiece and hung it with wallpaper imitating Dutch tiles.

The French Revolution encouraged the English to purchase wholesale dispersed collections of Sèvres. The Prince Regent – later George IV – joined in, aided and abetted by his French confectioner, along with the 3rd Marquess of Hertford and Beau Brummell; the Rothschilds too were avid collectors (Waddesdon, in Buckinghamshire, still contains much Sèvres). Hertford was one of the five generations of the Hertford family – the 1st to 4th Marquess, and the 4th Marquess's illegitimate son, Richard Wallace – who from the 1780s to the 1880s put together the Wallace Collection, now in London. It boasts the finest Sèvres museum collection in the world, which is displayed not by chronology but colour-coded.

The freestanding china cabinet, always in oriental style, started to appear in the 1750s, usually in women's bedrooms or closets. It took Josiah Wedgwood to bring ceramics into the state apartments again, with his more masculine, neo-classical forms and their ungilded simple colours. The third quarter of the eighteenth century was the heyday for society's interest in all kinds of porcelain, though this was also when oriental china – now cheaper and more plentiful – went out of favour. Ceramics continued to be displayed on fireplaces and door cornices into the early nineteenth century, when hanging wall shelves were invented. By the end of the nineteenth century the china cabinet was ubiquitous. China objects were also perched above bookcases around grand nineteenth-century rooms, as at Eaton Hall after its 1882 refurbishment, and in the more urban surroundings of Linley Sanbourne House in Kensington.

Perhaps the greatest English ceramics collectors of the nineteenth century were Lady Charlotte and Charles Schreiber, whose 1,800-strong collection of eighteenth-century English porcelain resides in the Victoria & Albert Museum. Lady Charlotte kept a detailed record of how it was put together between 1869 and 1882, which was published as 'Journals: confidences of a collector of ceramics and antiques' (1911). It tells of 'the search, the joy of possession, the discovery of the long-sought rarity that fills a gap . . .' In 1884 Charles died, whereupon Lady Charlotte lost interest in collecting.

The point about a collection is that it should be a living thing. Which is why the *way* we display ceramics is so important. By putting them on view in kitchens and other rooms for living in, we can receive constant pleasure. 'Ceramics for the Home' is dedicated to that cause.

# ancient & blue

**blue-and-white porcelain, delftware, transfer-printed pottery**

To the late twentieth-century collector, blue-and-white china is a familiar and reassuring friend. It was not always thus. Several hundred years before Willow Pattern waved its catkin fronds and blue cows grazed on Staffordshire soup bowls, blue-and-white had a fiercely exotic appeal to Europeans: inky designs scrolling around long-necked, gleaming white Chinese vases spoke of a country and culture unimaginably remote and strange.

It was the beginning of a love affair that has endured ever since. Millions of pieces of oriental porcelain were shipped to Europe and America between the early seventeenth and late nineteenth centuries, the majority of them blue-and-white. They were joined by a host of whimsical tin-glaze European imitations and, from the late eighteenth century, transfer-printed wares and blue-and-white spongeware. Indeed, each time a new kind of ceramic has been devised, it has for reasons technical and economical first been blue and white. The history of blue-and-white is therefore interlinked with the story of china itself.

Happily, the result of such productiveness is an abundance of antique blue-and-white, of an enormous variety of themes and styles, but much at affordable prices. And one of the many joyous features of blue-and-white is that because it almost all uses the same blue colourant (cobalt), every type seems to go well together.

Blue-and-white makes a strong but not overpowering statement. It stands out fresh and lustrous amongst the gilt and elaborate workmanship of a palace, yet looks equally striking in a country cottage. Types range from rare and expensive fifteenth-century Ming porcelain jars standing several feet high (around £500,000) to the everyday and affordable T.G. Green's striped Cornish Ware (about £6.50 a mug). Blue-and-white unites ancient and modern collector: the Sun King, Louis XIV of France, was one; Claude Monet ate off the stuff in his yellow kitchen-cum-dining room at Giverny; while the fashion designer Valentino is a current enthusiast.

## Cobalt – the essential ingredient

Blue is a hugely attractive colour, airily suggesting sky and sea. That is not, however, the only reason for its success in pottery form. It is rather because cobalt blue is the pigment that works best when used as an underglaze, on low-fired earthenware and high-fired porcelain alike.

Cobalt is a rare metal rather like nickel, used to produce high-grade steel and nuclear power. Cobalt oxide is mixed with oil or water to produce a paint which is black when applied but changes to inky blue when fired: 'the fire makes it appear in all its beauty, almost in the same way as the natural heat of the sun makes the most beautiful butterflies, with all their tints, come out of their eggs,' wrote Père d'Entrecolles, a Jesuit missionary living in China in the early eighteenth century. After being painted or printed on to dry clay, it is given a glassy glaze which, when fired, turns transparent and protects and preserves the colour.

Cobalt was first used on Middle Eastern ceramics in the ninth century and as an underglaze in late twelfth-century Persia. A hundred years on the technique and the ore were brought to China. Porcelain had been made in China since the Tang dynasty (618-906 AD). Its unique vitreousness and translucence were achieved by baking a mixture of kaolin (white china clay) and petuntse (china stone, a crystalline rock also used in the glaze) at an extremely high temperature, above 1300° C (2370°F). This temperature restricted the underglaze palette to cobalt blue and a strong but less reliable copper red.

## Chinese blue-and-white

By the start of the fifteenth century Chinese blue-and-white was fully developed technically and artistically. Pieces filtered through the Arab world to

*left:* the upside-down helmet shape of this early eighteenth-century faience Rouen helmet ewer was copied from silverware and its pendant *lambrequin* decoration from engraved French baroque designs. *right:* delftware kraak-style dish, c. 1810. Ming kraak ware, with its radial panels and central scene, was the first porcelain mass-produced for Europe in the early seventeenth century; it was named after the Dutch word for carrack, a merchant ship. Many delftware copies were made.

Guercino
257

269

Europe where they were regarded with awe: the Sultan of Egypt gave blue-and-white porcelain to the Doge of Venice and Lorenzo de' Medici. During this time travellers were venturing ever further outside Europe in search of trade routes. In 1497 Vasco da Gama pushed round the Cape of Good Hope; less than 20 years later, Portuguese ships sailed into Chinese waters and trade with the West started in earnest. Up until the end of the sixteenth century the Portuguese had the field to themselves. After that, the Dutch and the English moved in.

*previous pages:* a pyramid of Chinese pots decks the corner fireplace in the Blue Silk Dressing Room at Burghley House. It was recreated in 1986 – the Victorians had ripped out all the chimney displays. A *garniture de cheminée* usually consists of alternate lidded baluster and flared pots; these mostly Kanxi ceramics, dating to the mid- to late seventeenth century, have different shapes but form an equally symmetrical pattern. The originator of this kind of display was Daniel Marot, decorator to William and Mary; several of his many-tiered chimney pieces are still at Hampton Court. *this page, above:* a London delftware plate, 1700-10; its mermaid subject is most unusual; *right:* double-gourd vase from the Transitional period, c. 1620-80, between the Ming and Qing dynasties, when people in narrative scenes began to appear for the first time regularly. It would have been produced for export, outside the control of the Imperial factories.

In 1579, the buccaneering English sailor Sir Francis Drake captured a Spanish galleon containing a cargo of porcelain in the Pacific; when he stopped to repair his ship, the 'Golden Hind', near San Francisco, a case of blue-and-white was lost overboard. It became the first Chinese porcelain in North America and fragments of Wanli blue-and-white still decorate the graves of the Miwok Indians who lived in that part of California at the time.

To begin with, Chinese porcelain in Europe was as rare as it was expensive, and pieces were often set in silver or gold. A friend of Erasmus claimed that a single piece was worth several slaves. It was only as it became more affordable in the seventeenth century that chinamania, the obsessional passion for Chinese blue-and-white, grew up, first at the courts, then in grand houses. This was in large part thanks to the activities of the English and Dutch East India Companies, founded in 1600 and 1602 respectively.

Chinamania began when the Dutch captured two porcelain-laden carracks bound for Lisbon, the 'San Yago' and the 'Santa Caterina', in 1602 and 1603 respectively. (Spain had a deeply resented invading force in Holland, and Portugal had incurred Dutch enmity by uniting with Spain.) The auction in Holland of the 150,000-piece cargo generated such excitement – purchasers included Henry IV of France and James I of England – that from then on, vast amounts of Chinese blue-and-white began to be brought back to Europe by the East India Companies, and used as decoration.

To Europeans used to cruder, friable ceramics, the fineness of oriental porcelain was a revelation. It was pure white, delicately thin and light, yet surprisingly strong. It had a pleasing slippery gloss, and came in refined shapes with sophisticated, painted decoration of such exotic subjects as trailing lotus blossom. Most of all, it was semi-translucent. Europe was mad for it, and spurred on by the prospect of high rewards its potters worked furiously to create a white ceramic with similar properties. The race turned into something of a marathon, however, both because the Chinese kept the recipe a secret, and because Europe apparently lacked the necessary ingredient, kaolin.

Chinese blue-and-white covers a period of some 600 years, during which methods of manufacture remained largely the same. Production can be divided into wares made for the home market, the Imperial court and the export market. All three are collected in the West. The most widespread antique blue-and-white is eighteenth- and nineteenth-century exportware, which was made in vast amounts, but whose date is not always apparent in its design. The Chinese were keen and effective copiests of their best wares at almost all periods. In the eighteenth century they reproduced quantities of blue-and-white 'Ming'.

**Ming dynasty (1368-1644)**: The porcelain industry in China was based at Jingdezhen, home of the Imperial factories throughout the Ming dynasty. Père d'Entrecolles claimed that 18,000 families of potters lived here, and 3,000 kilns burnt day and night.

The earliest blue-and-white to reach Europe dates largely from the reign of the last great Ming emperor, Wanli (1573-1619). Wanli porcelain is thin and often moulded, its decoration veering from purply blue to pale silvery grey, particularly towards the end of the era. The occasional

*above:* a neat and balanced – though not symmetrical – arrangement of transfer-printed tureen lids stands out cheerfully against a yellow kitchen wall in mid-west France. They were picked up in junk shops by an English couple who run the house as a hotel.

*right:* a satisfyingly overall if higgledy-piggledy pattern of blue-and-white Chinese plates – including broken eighteenth-century armorial ones – and more ordinary domestic crockery, impressed into plaster in this gothic dairy in Surrey around 1900.

application of too much cobalt caused small black spots to appear through the glaze ('heaping and piling'), an effect later prized and imitated.

Exported ware was similar to that made for home consumption, along with some shapes favoured by the Islamic market. It was decorated with typical Ming motifs: dragons, cranes, peonies, lotuses, chrysanthemums and pagodas, each with a particular meaning. Cranes, for example, symbolised longevity, while dragons with five claws represented the emperor.

The first Chinese porcelain made specially for the European market was *kraak porselein* (named after the Dutch word for carrack), examples of which were in the captured Portuguese ships. It was painted with eight to twelve alternately wide and narrow radial panels containing animals, flowers or Buddhist symbols around a central scene, such as a bird on a rock or a deer. Quantities of kraak dishes were imported from the late sixteenth to the mid-seventeenth century. Even so, kraak ware is expensive.

**Transitional ware**: Of better quality than most kraak porcelain – though overlapping with it – was the ware made between the 1620s and the 1680s, later termed Transitional period because it bestrides the end of the Ming and the start of the Manchu or Qing dynasty. Such pieces were produced outside the control of the court – which had stopped ordering porcelain – often in private factories. The blue was deeper than

*left:* Rudolf Chotek was trade minister, then Chancellor of the Austro-Hungarian Empire in the mid-eighteenth century, when he created his delft dining room at Veltrusy in Bohemia; it contains both delft and oriental ceramics. *right:* Chinese and Japanese porcelain adorns the gilded mirror walls of the Porzellankabinett at Schloss Charlottenburg in Berlin. It was designed in the first decade of the eighteenth century, when the fashion for porcelain rooms was at its height; the room was destroyed in the Second World War but recreated in the 1950s.

before, with a violet hue. Instead of stylised motifs, naturalistic landscapes abound and even people in narrative scenes. Subjects were still purely Chinese, apart from the odd Dutch tulip, but the range of objects made widened to include such European staples as mustard pots, candlesticks and tankards.

When the Ming dynasty fell in the 1640s a civil war ensued. The importation of ceramics into Europe was severely curtailed until the 1690s. Production was gleefully stepped up in Delft, and the Dutch also began to trade with Japan – which had mastered porcelain-making early in the century – commissioning imitation wares from Arita until the Chinese market reopened. Thanks to its scarcity and high quality, Transitional ware tends to be expensive.

**The Qing dynasty (1644-1912)**: In 1683 the second Qing emperor, Kangxi (who ruled 1662-1722) took charge of the ceramic works at Jingdezhen, and the following year four ports, one of them Canton (for European companies), opened to foreign trade. It was an exciting time for the porcelain industry. Exports to the West multiplied, while an enormous repertoire of new objects based on European earthenware and silverware was introduced. Kangxi blue-and-white is technically superb. Its white body has a faint bluish or greenish tint and its blue decoration is luminous. Among the most admired wares were lidded, baluster-shaped prunus-blossom jars decorated with white sprigs of plum blossom against a rich blue 'cracked-ice' ground. They have been much copied.

*right:* the porcelain kitchen at Thureholm in Sweden was given its fanciful chinoiserie decoration in the 1740s, when such a style was the height of fashion. Its painted shelves and consoles were designed to show off the family's collection of blue-and-white Chinese export porcelain, some of which is now at the Skansen Open-air Museum, Stockholm. There are 125 buildings at Skansen, among them Skogaholm, a restored Gustavian manor from Närke, whose kitchen (*above*) contains racks of eighteenth-century faience by Rörstrand.

Also produced in great numbers during the Qing dynasty were *garnitures de cheminée* – sets of contrasting baluster and flared blue-and-white vases sold in groups of three, five or seven and used to decorate a chimney piece with elegant formality. In the late 1980s, a poor Vietnamese fisherman snagged his nets on the submerged wreck of the 'Vung Tau', a local ship sunk in the late seventeenth century on its way from the coastal Chinese potteries to the Dutch headquarters in Java. Much of its 28,000-strong blue-and-white cargo consisted of sets of pristine vases dating from 1690 and made for the European market. These were sold at Christie's in Amsterdam in 1992. Oriental blue-and-white vases still make a handsome decoration. The standard set consists of three large lidded jars and two trumpet-shaped vases. A small-scale garniture can be made cheaply from remnants of services or reproductions.

**The East India Companies**

Throughout the seventeenth century, the supply of Chinese porcelain to Europe was largely controlled by the Dutch East India Company. Shiploads would arrive at Rotterdam and Antwerp, and it was in Holland at the tail end of the seventeenth century that the fashion for blue-and-white roomscapes first emerged. The English East India Company's main trading partner was India, but trade with China was increased after 1715 when it established its own trading post on the Chinese mainland – joined over a decade later by the French, the Dutch, the Danes and the Swedes.

The English East India Company also controlled the American porcelain market until after the American Civil War. Wares shipped to settlers there were similar to those imported into Europe, though more in the Chinese taste. When American ship owners started to deal with Canton direct in 1784 their keenness for oriental porcelain revitalised the export market. By the early nineteenth century, the United States was its dominant customer. Blue-and-white popular in early nineteenth-century America included Canton ginger jars (similar to Kangxi prunus-blossom jars) and Canton, a dinner service decorated with a pale Willow Pattern-like landscape. By the 1830s, however, American potteries were producing their own robust tableware, and interest in Chinese porcelain declined.

Porcelain was an attractive cargo for practical as well as mercantile reasons. Unlike tea, spices, silk, ivory and lacquer, it could be placed in a wet hold since sea water did no damage to it. Being heavy it was also good as ballast, and made a vessel stable when packed tightly in the hold.

The enormous amount of tableware brought back to Europe eventually brought down its price. Chinese blue-and-white became as cheap as delftware. Europe's table habits changed too. Whereas in the sixteenth century porcelain had been far too precious to eat off, by the early eighteenth century, anyone who could afford to ate off Chinese porcelain. Rich Englishmen commissioned dinner services from China adorned with their crests or coats of arms. Until 1730 these were made only in blue-and-white.

### Eighteenth- and nineteenth-century Chinese porcelain

In the early 1700s, 40,825 kg (90,000 lb) of tea a year were imported to England. By 1800 this had risen to 20,412,000 kg (45,000,000 lb). The great European surge of tea- and coffee-drinking demanded new vessels from which to sip the beverages. Delicate blue-and-white teabowls from the Far East, like the tea, fitted the bill perfectly. Teacups were introduced in around 1780.

By now, Chinese porcelain faced competition from the European variety. Colossal tax increases were imposed on imported porcelain to help the home markets. More devastating still was the introduction around 1765 of Josiah Wedgwood's new clay body, creamware (cream-coloured earthenware composed of ground flint and white pipeclay with a silky lead glaze), which was attractive, hard-wearing and cheap. It swiftly became the standard domestic pottery for England and much of the world. By 1791 the English East India Company had stopped buying bulk chinaware (then some 2,000,000 pieces a year) to allow more room for tea.

From the mid-eighteenth century the standard of porcelain exported from China deteriorated. Nineteenth-century blue-and-white, known in America and England as Nanking ware, was of vastly inferior quality, though unpretentious.

*above:* airy blue-and-white curtains frame and enhance the busy still life of blue-and-white Chinese export porcelain – collected piece by piece – in the Grand Salon of a Normandy *folie*. This *mise-en-scène*, like the design of the curtains' fabric, was put together by the costume historian, house collector and decorator Lillian Williams.

*above:* a mixture of Chinese, English, Dutch and Persian ceramics united by their cobalt hues, in a London drawing room.
*right:* an elegantly cool display of late Ming porcelain in the dining room of a Belgian castle near Antwerp. The vases came from the 'Hatcher Junk', a shipwreck of 1643-46 salvaged in the early 1980s. (Captain Michael Hatcher later found the eighteenth-century Dutch East Indiaman 'Geldermalsen' – the Nanking Cargo – which caused even more of a stir). White walls, furniture and a pale marble floor emphasise the pallid effect, while the painted brackets echo the shape of the Dutch corner cupboard.

## Historic collections

An early spectacular display of blue-and-white was Queen Mary II of England's 'Delft-Ware Closet' at Hampton Court. Its walls were a riot of jars and vases along mantelpieces, around doors and on any number of specially built brackets. As wife of William of Orange, Mary (1662-1694) had created porcelain rooms both in The Hague and at her country house in Honsselarsdijk. (Her tiled room at Paleis Het Loo can be seen today.) Her collection embraced Dutch and oriental blue-and-white, including seventeenth-century Japanese ware.

The man responsible for these displays was Daniel Marot (1663-1752), a Huguenot who had fled persecution in France to Holland, where he worked for William and Mary before moving to England when they became king and queen in 1689. His engraved schemes for houses give ornate suggestions for displaying china. In one illustration there are more than 300 pieces of china on the chimney piece alone.

As queen, Mary encouraged the fashion for blue-and-white in England. Daniel Defoe wrote disapprovingly in 'A Tour Through the Whole Island of Great Britain':

> The queen brought in the custom or humour, as I might call it, of furnishing Houses with china-ware, which spread to lesser mortals and increased to a strange degree afterwards, piling their china upon the tops of cabinets, scrutores, and every chymneypiece, to the tops of the ceilings, and even setting up shelves for their china-ware where they wanted such places, till it became a grievance in the expense of it and even injurious to their families and estates.

Pictures of grand china rooms around Europe confirm the extremes to which the style was taken but also the effectiveness of composing in blue-and-white masses. Of blue-and-white porcelain rooms still extant, perhaps the most thrilling is at Schloss Charlottenburg in Berlin. It was designed for the Court of Brandenburger and completed in 1706. Though destroyed during the Second World War it was recreated in the 1950s with a new collection of small vases perched on brackets framing mirror-glass panels.

*left:* a busy display of nineteenth-century transfer wares on a half-dresser, collected by Kate Dyson of the Dining Room Shop in London. A few large dishes balance crowded rows of smaller sugar shakers, eye baths and mugs. Gleaming white and inky blue is excellently set off by warm golds and browns, whether a twentieth-century American animal-theme service on a tawny painted dresser (*right*), or the parade of mostly Kangxi Chinese vases and bottles at Calke Abbey, Derbyshire (*below left*) against a backdrop of large-scale flock-pattern wallpaper; the large vase at the back is mid-seventeeenth century Arita in the Ming style.

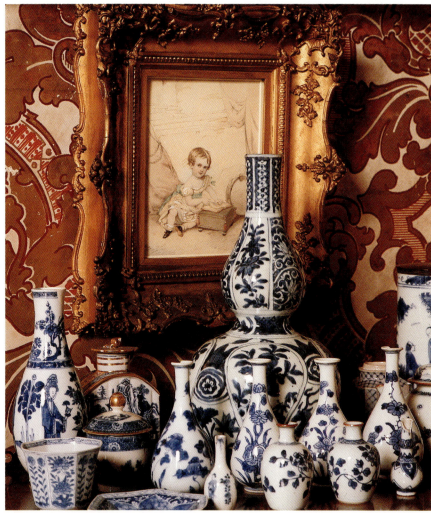

## Aesthetic revival in England

Blue-and-white enjoyed something of a revival in mid-nineteenth-century England, thanks to the Aesthetic Movement's passion for blue-and-white porcelain, which was termed 'blue', and treated with theatrical veneration. The writer Andrew Lang, in 'Ballades in Blue China' (1880), summed up blue's heady merits:

There's a joy without canker or cark,

There's a pleasure eternally new,

'Tis to gloat on the glaze and the mark

Of china that's ancient and blue;

Unchipp'd all the centuries through

It has pass'd, since the chime of it rang,

And they fashion'd it, figure and hue,

In the reign of the Emperor Hwang.

Blue's chief champion was the painter James Abbott McNeill Whistler (1834-1903). One of his most famous paintings, 'The Little White Girl', contains 'blue', while his 'Rose and Silver: The Princess from the Land of Porcelain' was hung at the centre of the shipping magnate F.R. Leyland's splendidly arrayed blue-porcelain collection against Spanish leather-lined walls. Leyland's china room evolved into Whistler's Peacock Room (see page 7), which today, decked with a new collection of blue, is at the Freer Gallery in Washington, DC.

The Pre-Raphaelite Dante Gabriel Rossetti was another influential fan of blue, while Oscar Wilde's first publicised *bon mot*, as an Oxford undergraduate, was allegedly, 'I find it harder and harder every day to live up to my blue china'. The Aesthetes' favourite shop, Liberty of London, promoted Willow Pattern and imported Kangxi-style ginger jars and trumpet vases.

## Tin-glazed earthenware: delftware and faience

Tin-glaze is a handsome white glaze made by adding tin oxide to transparent lead glaze. Earthenware was first dipped in tin glaze in ninth-century Baghdad – mimicking white Chinese porcelain even then. Several centuries on, tin-glazed earthenware appeared in Europe, called maiolica in Italy, delftware in Holland and England, and faience everywhere else. From the seventeenth century on, it was frequently painted with blue decorations before firing, in response to the frenzied desire for oriental blue-and-white.

Of all the cheaper imitations of porcelain, the best and most successful was produced from about 1600 in the town of Delft in Holland. Delftware was made of a local buff-coloured clay and was given a glossy lead glaze known as *kwaart* before the final firing, to imitate the high sheen of Chinese porcelain. So popular was it, that Delft became the centre of the ceramic industry in Europe and was replaced only at the close of the

*left:* a Liverpool tin-glazed stoneware teapot, c. 1755-60 – an unusual combination of body and glaze. *below:* late seventeenth- and early eighteenth-century Dutch Delftwares, including whimsical shoes and multi-spouted tulip vases – tulipmania and chinamania had coincided in the early seventeenth century. At Hampton Court pagoda-shaped tulip vases several feet high were commissioned by William and Mary.

eighteenth century – thanks to creamware and transfer-printing – by Staffordshire. It was particularly celebrated for its blue-and-white tiles.

Under the sway of porcelain, delftware became finer and its decoration more delicate, while the backs as well as the fronts of dishes were glazed. However, unlike Chinese porcelain (which was fired only once, at a greater heat), delftware was liable to chip and stain – and it was far from translucent. (Indeed, damage is so widespread it has little effect on the price of delftware – unlike most other kinds of china.)

Chinese designs were Delft's most popular decoration, at first exact copies from Chinese porcelain and later chinoiseries. By the 1690s huge European shapes were being attempted, like the tall, multi-spouted tulip vases in the shape of obelisks or pagodas at Hampton Court Palace, commissioned by William and Mary. Delftware was turned into useful and decorative objects alike – including up-to-the-minute novelties such as bird cages and miniature shoes. Delft's golden age was from the mid-seventeenth to the mid-eighteenth century; after that its demise was swift; only two Delft factories survived into the nineteenth century.

**European delftware and faience outside Holland**: Tin-glazed earthenware flourished in France from the late sixteenth century. At Rouen, embroidery-like blue-and-white *style rayonnant* decoration evolved, along with an elegant painting style inspired by the court designer Jean Bérain's 'grotesque' engravings of scrollwork, acanthus foliage and *lambrequins*. The potteries at Moustiers and Marseilles in the south followed suit.

Blue-and-white delftware was the most common crockery in England in the first half of the eighteenth century; every large town had at least one pottery. The major centres were Bristol and Liverpool and, in London, Aldgate, Southwark and Vauxhall. While English delft has a duller finish and a coarser body and glaze than Dutch Delft, its sketchy landscapes and stylised figures, mixing Chinese and English motifs, have a naive charm. It enjoyed a late flowering in the later eighteenth century, just as it was being driven out of the market by creamware.

*previous pages:* blue-and-white china in two sets of shelves in niches. The well-ordered one on the left is in the Still Room at Traquair House in Peeblesshire; the octagonal Chinese Export plates and other pieces look chic and neat against a rich blue background. By contrast, the crowded shelves on the right contain more of a mixture of types and shapes of china but, thanks to the unifying shade of blue, still look attractive.

In Germany, factories at Hanau, Frankfurt, Berlin, Nuremberg, Potsdam and Kassel all imitated Dutch Delft. Even in Spain, Talavera pottery succumbed to Ming and Delft influences in the late seventeenth century. The main Scandinavian faience factories, like Rörstrand in Sweden (founded 1728), produced only blue-painted wares in their first years of production.

## European porcelain

The first porcelain developed in Europe was 'soft' rather than 'hard' paste like the Chinese. It was made from a mixture of white clay and ground glass fired at a lower temperature than its Chinese counterpart. In the late seventeenth century, experiments by French faiencemakers led to the manufacture of a creamy soft-paste at Rouen and later Saint-Cloud, Tournai and Chantilly, which was often blue-decorated. Then, thrillingly, in 1708 at Meissen, a young alchemist, Johann Friedrich Böttger (1682-1719) made his first version of hard paste (a closely guarded secret) using kaolin mined in Germany. Little blue-and-white was made at Meissen during the eighteenth century, except for a few tablewares such as Onion (designed by Johann Gregor Herold), which is still made today.

In England soft-paste porcelain was developed at the Chelsea, Bow, Worcester, Derby and Longton Hall factories in the 1740s and 1750s. While their Continental counterparts enjoyed royal patronage and subsidies, English porcelain factories were commercial ventures which depended entirely on the sale of their wares. Blue-and-white was swiftly adopted as a staple product. It required just one firing (multicoloured enamel wares needed several) and sold at comparable prices to the Chinese porcelain it imitated.

Shapes were mainly derived from silverware, and because soft-paste tended to warp, quantities of small items such as tea wares and pickle dishes were made. Worcester was the biggest producer. The bulk of its output was decorated with oriental designs in underglaze blue and later with romanticised

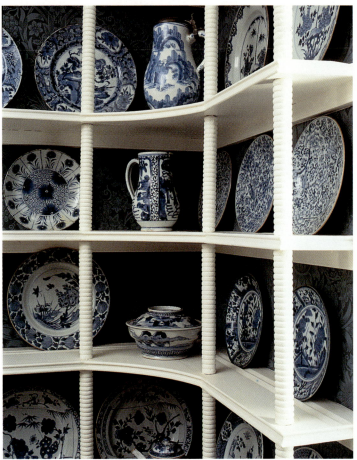

landscapes and floral patterns. Made to a secret formula using Cornish soaprock, Worcester porcelain was well suited for tea services: it did not stain, was durable (unlike softer paste Bow) and withstood boiling tea.

Bow, which for a time styled itself New Canton, also made quantities of oriental-style blue-and-white – some to Worcester patterns – which it exported heavily to North America. The Caughley (pronounced 'car flea') factory in Shropshire began making porcelain after 1772. Many of its designs, such as Pine Cone, were 'borrowed' from Worcester. There were other factories with a strong blue-and-white output in Vauxhall, and several in Liverpool.

*previous pages, main picture:* blue-and-white checked chair covers complement the strong-hued, mostly early nineteenth-century transfer ware ranged round antique dealer Jonathan Vickers' dining room; *top left:* old and new blue-and-white – Japanese, Persian, Bleu de Fès from Morocco, and nineteenth-century Staffordshire wares in alcoves splashed blue to imitate pottery from the Gemundener Keramik factory in Austria; *below left:* white-painted barley-sugar-supports in the pantry designed by Philip Webb for William Morris at Kelmscott Manor, set off the glossy oriental blue-and-white. *this page, above:* a transfer-printed plate in the intense blue popular in 1820s America; the thick floral border was also typical of the period.

Lowestoft in Suffolk, set up in 1757 after fine clay was discovered in the area, produced a charming blue-painted white paste, largely for the local East Anglian market, until 1802. At first wares were decorated in a loose Chinese style, but soon seaside or commemorative inkwells and mugs marked 'A Trifle from Lowestoft' and decorated with, for example, a bathing machine, were also made, as were copies of Worcester.

**Transfer-printed wares**

In the second half of the eighteenth century the ceramic industry was revolutionised both by the introduction of Wedgwood's creamware and by the use of prints as decoration. This first happened at the Battersea Enamel Factory in 1753. By the end of the decade underglaze blue transfer-prints were being applied to porcelain at Worcester and Bow. Ten years on the majority of wares were printed rather than hand-painted. In 1780 the first transfer-printed earthenware was made at Caughley; four years later Spode had perfected the technique. Designs were engraved on copper plates, which were then inked up and transferred to paper. While the colour was still wet the paper was carefully positioned on the ceramic. The technique has remained unchanged since around 1810, with some original copper plates still being used today.

Early on, a group of distressed enamel painters beseeched Josiah Wedgwood to help stop transfer-printing, which was putting them out of business. He promised he would never make blue-printed wares, and he never did. Wedgwood's first, the Chinese Vase Pattern, appeared eleven years after his death, in 1806. During the first quarter of the nineteenth century, transfer-printing became the standard method of decorating cheaper wares, sometimes in brown and other colours (as at Creil, the first French pottery to produce transfer wares), but usually in blue. A host of small firms turned out Chinese-style patterns, both in Staffordshire and in factories in Leeds, Newcastle and Liverpool in the North, and Bristol and Swansea in the West. From early on, blue-and-white's new incarnation was exported around the world – increasingly so after the Napoleonic Wars.

Transfer wares literally dish up art on a plate: handsome scenes transferred from engravings to smallish, often round, ceramic areas. The sculptural element of the china is unimportant. What matters is the print's two-dimensional crispness or narrative. This is why such ceramics work well on a wall.

**Transfer ware for the American market**: As the eighteenth century drew to a close myriad transfer-ware designs appeared which were not 'Chinese' but taken from books of picturesque engravings, depicting, for example, India, romantic ruins or grand buildings. These were greatly sought after by the American market, which by the 1810s was dominant. A whole genre depicting historic American scenes sprang up. One of the most successful exporters to the US was Enoch Wood, who produced 58 American views, around 80 English ones and 11 French. Minton's Oxford and Cambridge colleges were popular on both sides of the Atlantic, while their Beauties of America featured noteworthy buildings on the East Coast. Wood introduced an intense dark blue – widely imitated – which Americans particularly favoured, along with borders composed of shells and flowers. The boom lasted 15 or so years, until the 1830s, at a time when blue-printed wares were often of superb quality.

**The Willow Pattern**: Chinoiserie patterns continued to be mass-produced throughout the nineteenth century, including the best-known blue-printed design, Willow Pattern,

an English invention based on Chinese themes. Numerous versions exist, but constant features include a willow tree, a tea house, a boat, a fence zigzagging across the foreground, an orange tree, three figures crossing the bridge and an island, above which soar two birds representing lovers. The earliest, in steely blue on porcelain, is the 'Caughley Willow Pattern'. This is often ascribed to Thomas Minton, then an apprentice engraver and later the founder of the Minton factory.

The first Staffordshire maker to use Willow Pattern, circa 1790, was Josiah Spode, from an original Chinese pattern called Mandarin. Spode's standard Willow Pattern was its third version, made from 1810. Willow Patterns were made at most nineteenth-century potteries and became more crowded as the century progressed, as did the geometrical rim. Hundreds of other designs also contain a willow tree. The potter Robert Dawson recently made a series of plates magnifying details of traditional Willow Pattern.

**Other transfer-ware patterns**: In the early nineteenth century, the border on transfer wares grew ever more luxuriant with motifs often taken from contemporary fabrics and wallpapers. By 1810 Davenport had introduced the heavy floral border so popular in the Regency era. Ralph Hall of Tunstall's Wild Rose Pattern, named after its broad border, proved second in popularity only to Willow Pattern between 1830 and 1855, and was re-produced by numerous potteries.

The most celebrated maker of blue-printed earthenware, Spode, introduced dozens of patterns in styles Greek, Italian and romantic, along with copies of Chinese porcelain. The Spode engravers were brilliant interpreters of picturesque prints: the Indian Sporting series was taken from the periodical 'Oriental Field Sports, Wild Sports of the East' (from 1805), and Italian views from Merigot's 'Views and Ruins in Rome and its Vicinity' (1797-98). The most commercially successful pattern was the romantic land-scape Italian, introduced in 1816 and still produced today.

Underglaze blue-printed Staffordshire earthenware remains one of the largest classes of pottery. During its first decades, the lack of copyright laws meant that many factories used identical prints, making their wares impossible to identify exactly. Furthermore, even factories like Davenport baulked at marking services of up to 200 pieces. This adds to collectors' fun. Look for quality in the engraving rather than a maker's mark. Remember that brighter and softer colours were introduced later on.

## Cornish Ware

Jaunty, striped Cornish Kitchen Ware was launched by T.G. Green in the 1920s and has remained popular ever since. It is alleged that Green's south of England representative named it after 'the blue of the Cornish skies and the white crests of the waves'. Its crisp lines and solid shapes cleverly make it appear functional, traditional and modern at the same time. It has something of the seaside about it, cries out to be used, and is triumphantly simple and decorative.

British potters had made banded slipware throughout the nineteenth century. In 1864 Thomas Goodwin Green bought a maker of no-nonsense utility wares in Church Gresley, Derbyshire. He built a new factory and introduced stripy mochaware and white hospital wares which were produced until the 1940s. By the 1920s T.G. Green employed 700 people – Cornish Ware may have been introduced to keep them busy during the Depression. Spotted Blue Domino Ware was added in around 1933.

Although the company struggled in the 1930s and 1940s, the Cornish Ware range continued to expand: bowls and squat jugs were joined by sugar shakers, egg cups, storage jars and even rolling pins. It enjoyed a thriving export market, especially to New Zealand and Australia, but also to Europe. Its best-known imitators are Staffordshire Chef Ware and Swinnerton's Somerset Blue.

From the late 1950s other colours were introduced, notably 'sunlit yellow' and Cornish Gold, but blue and white remained the most popular. In the late 1960s its shapes were redesigned by Judith Onions, and these are still manufactured today.

*previous pages:* an airy display of blue-and-white in a Cambridgeshire larder; its owner collects anything blue and white, new or old, as long as it is decorative. *facing page:* two of Robert Dawson's 1996 set of seven plates using giant elements of the traditional Willow Pattern to create a smart, modern design; *below:* Cornish Ware jugs by T.G. Green, first produced in the 1920s and still made today.

# floral & botanical

**the depiction of flowers, foliage, fruit and vegetables in ceramic form**

The association of polite floral teacups with elderly aunts should not blind collectors to the often exotic joys of petals, plants and pottery. Natural forms have an uncontrived *joie de vivre*. Like flowers and fruit themselves, even the humblest piece of botanically decked china looks good in a domestic setting. A cabbage-shaped tureen is a frilled sculptural splendour, while a couple of pink floral plates in the midst of green majolica introduce a delicate burst of colour that enhances the other objects.

Stylised floral motifs appear on Ancient Egyptian, medieval Islamic and the earliest Chinese ceramics alike. In Europe, the delight in rendering tender blooms, foliage, fruits and even vegetables on china (or in ceramic form) reached full-flowering in the eighteenth and early nineteenth centuries. This was the age of plant hunters, when the Swedish botanist Carl von Linné (Linnaeus) laid down the rules for plant nomenclature, and gorgeously coloured botanical prints proliferated. What better than to team these fragile natural wonders with enamel colours and new-fangled ceramics, namely porcelain and creamware?

## Meissen *Blumen*

The first European porcelain maker to depict flowers was Meissen. In the 1720s a Meissen painter, Johann Gregor Herold, made a new floral decoration using aspects of Japanese Kakiemon and Chinese *famille verte* in the collection of the factory's first patron, Augustus the Strong. He adapted the asymmetry, the outlined petals and iron red, smoky blue, green and yellow palette of Kakiemon to Meissen's own baroque forms. The style was (perversely) christened *Indianische Blumen* (Indian flowers) and was swiftly taken up in France, Italy and England.

By 1740 *Indianische Blumen* had been superseded at Meissen by the more naturalistic *Deutsche Blumen* (German flowers) based on contemporary botanical prints, this time with no discernible outlines, but shading and some insects. Also keenly copied, in particular at Höchst, Vincennes (and later Sèvres), Chelsea, Worcester and Derby, *Deutsche Blumen* was a joyful, sophisticated art.

left: a Bow leaf-shaped dish, c. 1755, with 'Quail' pattern; its decoration mimics that of late seventeenth-century Japanese Kakiemon porcelain which, when it was adapted at Meissen in the 1720s, became the first European floral ceramic style, *Indianische Blumen*. This was succeeded by the more naturalistic *Deutsche Blumen* (*detail, above*), then in England by full-blooded botanical painting, as in this Chelsea Hans Sloane soup-plate depicting a fritillary (*right*), c. 1756, complete with bugs, butterflies and a pupa.

## Botanical specimens

The English took *Deutsche Blumen* a stage further and made a speciality of painting bold and lovingly precise individual flowers on porcelain. Chelsea's celebrated Hans Sloane flower plates set the trend in about 1755. Sloane was a botanist and collector whose treasures formed the basis of the British Museum. The plates' flowers were alleged to have been based on his specimens, but the strong designs in heightened colours actually seem to have been taken from prints by the botanical artist George Ehret and Philip Miller, curator of the Chelsea Physic Garden. Decorative effect triumphs, and in some cases leaves have been transplanted from one species to another to boost the composition. Subjects range from auriculas and crown imperials to turnips and swedes, and frequently possess woody roots as well as more conventionally lovely flower heads. Chelsea botanical porcelain is fiendishly expensive. Striking reproductions are made by the American company Mottahedeh.

Another important botanical service, Royal Copenhagen's Flora Danica, consists of 1,500 pieces, each one painted with a Danish wild plant. Begun in 1790 for Catherine the Great of Russia but completed only in 1802, after her death, it was kept by the King of Denmark and is now at Rosenborg Castle, Copenhagen. A second set was made for the marriage of Princess Alexandra of Denmark to the Prince of Wales (later Edward VII) in 1863. Reproductions are still available.

Most of the major porcelain factories of the eighteenth and early nineteenth centuries produced botanical ware, as did manufacturers of creamware such as Wedgwood and Swansea. Of modern services that draw on botanical prints, perhaps the most

distinctive is Botanic Garden, launched in 1972 by Portmeirion. Its printed designs on earthenware come from nineteenth-century volumes such as 'Stephenson and Churchill's Medical Botany' and are very reasonably priced.

## Full-blown flowers

Flower-painted tea and dessert services in porcelain, creamware and pottery were produced throughout Europe. Until the late eighteenth century, apart from botanical painting, most flowers on china were tame and standardised: perfectly pretty but pretty lifeless. In England, the emergence of William Billingsley (1758-1828) and others at Derby ensured that floral depiction progressed in a far more sensual and full-blown manner.

Billingsley was apprenticed at the age of 16. He developed a way of representing flowers that made them look tender and lifelike. His specialities were fulsome pink roses, bouquets and naturalistic border patterns, all painted from life. His technique was like oil painting: after applying thick enamel pigment he wiped out the highlights so the background white porcelain showed through. This became standard practice in England. Billingsley grew increasingly preoccupied with developing his own china body and in 1796 left Derby to set up Pinxton. Thus began two decades of moving from factory to factory, attempting to create a permanent outlet for the white soft-paste he had devised, which won many admirers but proved unsuccessful financially. During this time he helped found Welsh porcelain at Swansea (where Thomas Pardoe was another fine flower painter) and Nantgarw, before ending up at Coalport.

After Billingsley left Derby, John Brewer and later William 'Quaker' Pegg (1775-1851) took over. Pegg was a brilliant china painter who on becoming a Quaker decided that his craft was frivolous, and for a long time gave it up. His full-size blooms drawn from life were less soft and feminine than Billingsley's. Examples include gloriously over-blown striped tulips, geraniums and sweetpeas.

*previous pages:* a garden of earthy delights in the dining room of textile maestro Kaffe Fassett. He designed it as a set for a book and liked it so much most of the props have stayed, from the repro verdure tapestry by Belinda Coote to the nineteenth-century majolica foliage plates from Britannia Antiques in London, which he added to his own leafy ceramics collection. *this page, above:* Derby dessert plate painted with honeysuckle in c. 1795 by William 'Quaker' Pegg. He was one of the factory's outstanding decorators; he always painted from life and his flowers are usually life-size.

## Sprigs and sprays

At the other end of the scale are delicate sprays of leaves and flowers that dot rather than dominate a piece. Many factories such as Tournai, Mennecy, Limoges and Vincennes-Sèvres produced these alongside more grandiose creations. Even today workaday prettiness rather than showy tours de force can seem more appropriate for daily tableware.

Chelsea turned out wares scattered with tiny bouquets. Stylised blue Chantilly sprays were popular in France and England, while the cornflower, or Angoulême sprig – simple sprays of blue flowers and green leaves – was one of the late eighteenth century's most widespread floral decorations, and was allegedly designed at Sèvres in 1782 to delight Marie-Antoinette. By this stage Sèvres had overtaken Meissen as the most imitated factory in Europe.

## Flowers and faience

France boasts a long tradition of flower-painting on faience. In the loveliest, eighteenth-century examples, exquisite painting is enhanced by subtle hues on a milky white body. Up until then, only certain colours could be attained because painters worked on the raw glaze, necessitating firing at a high temperature (*grand feu*). By painting on an already fired glaze, it was possible to cook enamel colours at a lower heat (*petit feu*) and to achieve rich colours – buttery yellow, dark blue, and a crimson-purple unknown to modern reproductions.

*Petit feu* was first practised at Strasbourg in the mid-eighteenth century. At around the same time, Meissen-trained Adam Friedrich von Löwenfinck

*top:* a scattering of Derby roses in the manner of the factory's first great flower painter, William Billingsley, 1820s. *above:* a more formal, neo-classical Sèvres Charles X botanical tazza painted by Jacques Sinsson, 1823-25. *right:* a faience Strasbourg plate, c. 1748, painted by Christian Wilhelm Löwenfinck with enamel *petit feu* colours – far more delicate than the ones obtainable using *grand feu* colours. The naturalistic flower painting introduced by the Löwenfinck brothers became known as *fleurs de Strasbourg.*

*above:* bold-coloured bird and botanical plates sing out from behind the glass and bars of a gothic-style bathroom cabinet in this former Greenwich docker's cottage. *right:* real and trompe-l'oeil Lunéville faience compete with each other in the writer June Ducas's sunlit dining room. The wallpaper, Lunéville Niche by Brunschwig & Fils, is based on an eighteenth-century pattern; the matching ceramics are a mixture of antiques and modern copies.

introduced naturalistic *Deutsche Blumen*, which became known as Strasbourg flowers and were taken up by other French faience factories. Naturalistic *grand feu* flowers had already appeared at the Marseilles factory, on white or yellow grounds, and were widely imitated. Other centres of fine floral faience production were Moustiers, Niderviller and Sceaux.

French faience is found largely in France, and its high-spirited delicacy makes it worth seeking out for bedroom and drawing room alike. Rural potteries in southern France continued to paint flower-strewn services throughout the nineteenth century, often in earlier styles. These can be tremendously decorative and are far cheaper than the originals.

### Nineteenth-century flowers

In nineteenth-century Europe the depiction of flowers kept giddy pace with changing decorative styles. The sober neo-classicism of the opening decades was followed by Revived Rococo, a flouncing feminine style inspired by the French rococo of the 1740s, in which bouquets of flowers on china featured prominently. By 1830 it was in full swing in France, England (at Rockingham, Derby, Davenport and Coalport), Bohemia and Russia.

Revived Rococo is not for the fainthearted. Its opulently decorated artefacts need space to flaunt their finery, enabling just one handsomely crafted piece to dominate a table, fireplace or room. By mid-century, it had given way to a mannered version of eighteenth-century Sèvres, in which strong turquoise and pink ground colours, gilding, and rose festoons became a familiar combination. It was the boast of Coalport and Minton that their Sèvres copies were indistinguishable from the real thing. French factories too turned out wares inspired by old Sèvres models.

*left:* full-blown pink roses on a bone china Ridgway teapot stand, c. 1820. The roses are of a kind pioneered at Derby in the late eighteenth century, with some background white porcelain showing through; the heavy gilding was a later fashion. *above:* Revived Rococo flower-encrusted Derby teataster of c. 1835. *below:* a more restrained 'rustic-style' stoneware Staffordshire teapot, c. 1765.

By the end of the century the international style was flowing Art Nouveau. Tall slender forms were adorned with sinuous plant-like patterns, and stylised flowers. In England, Moorcroft fashioned Freesia, Orchid and Florian patterns. Art Nouveau's greatest ceramic exponent, the Rozenburg factory in The Hague, made tapering egg-shell porcelain decorated with elongated flowers. At Rookwood and the Newcomb College Pottery in America, irises, gardenias and other plants were depicted in soulful greens and blacks.

## Modelled flowers

Flower-encrusted objects are deliciously excessive and textured. Putting one in a minimalist environment would create too extreme a discrepancy for comfort, let alone pleasure. A gorgeous gilded ambience would set it off perfectly.

Like many types of ceramics, porcelain flowers were first made by Meissen in the early decades of the eighteenth century. When Marie-Josèphe of Saxony married the Dauphin of France, she took the fashion with her, and by the mid-1740s there were 45 women at Vincennes making porcelain flowers. In 1749, Marie-Josèphe presented her father, Augustus III, with a bouquet of 480 ceramic flowers (today in the Dresden Museum). Around the same time, Madame de Pompadour received the king in mid-winter at Bellevue before a bank of porcelain blooms sprayed with different scents.

Most ceramic flowers were mounted on brass stems and used to embellish chandeliers, vases and wall sconces. Derby, Bow and Worcester made pierced frill vases (for pot-pourri) adorned with a leafy 'frill' and modelled flowers. Meissen studded

*previous pages, left:* columns of Scottish majolica, c. 1890, flank the drawing-room mirror at Old Mayen, a seventeenth-century Scottish hall house; *right:* American majolica plates hang above majolica sweetcorn and pineapple jugs in a contemporary setting in a house in Topanga Canyon, Los Angeles. *this page, below:* a Wemyss-ware loving cup decorated with cherries, c. 1900; *right:* a cluster of nineteenth-century French porcelain carnations, dahlias and other flower heads; each petal was modelled separately, then put together.

vases and tea sets with small white flowers, some gathered into big balls (hence the name *Schneeballen*, 'snowballs'). The style spread around Europe.

In nineteenth-century England, Minton smothered vases, tea wares, even figures with flower heads. Rockingham made flower-encrusted scent bottles and Coalport applied blossoms most abundantly of all, along with moulded rococo forms, foliage handles and rich flower painting. These objects are over the top and great fun.

## Wemyss ware

The simple shapes, boldly painted fruit and flowers and green scallop-edged trim that characterise Wemyss ware make it unpretentious yet smart, suitable for both kitchen and drawing room. It is a Scottish product made with Bohemian flair.

In around 1882 the Fife Pottery, Kirkcaldy, brought Karl Nekola (died 1915), a craft painter, over from Austria. Nekola introduced Wemyss's trademark cottage-style cabbage roses, hens and fruit on large ewers and basins, cats, pigs and popular jam pots. The range was christened Wemyss ware after Lady Henry Grosvenor of Wemyss Castle. Similar wares were produced by the nearby pottery of David Methven and Sons and, from the early 1900s, by the Pountney Pottery Co of Bristol. When production in Kirkaldy stopped in 1930, the Bovey Tracey pottery in Devon bought the rights and moulds, and Nekola's son Joseph continued to paint Wemyss ware decorations until his death in 1942.

### Fruit and vegetables

Naturalistic ceramic fruit and vegetables were a rococo amusement at Meissen and Chelsea, where cabbage and artichoke tureens were created, along with dishes in the form of asparagus, cauliflowers, melons and other produce. In the 1760s, some of Josiah Wedgwood's earliest pieces were superbly detailed press-moulded cauliflowerware, pineapple coffeepots and apple and pear teapots. Meissen and Chelsea wares were widely copied by German and French faience manufacturers such as Strasbourg and Marseilles. Modern imitations are convincing and cheap.

*right:* a hot array of American novelty ceramic tomatoes. *below right:* majolica leaves flutter over nineteenth-century Chinese stoneware fruit – sometimes used as temple offerings – in a New York flat. *far right:* English porcelain leaves and vegetables line this Georgian bookcase in a flat in Sydney, Australia. They include eighteenth-century Chelsea and Longton Hall leaf plates and sauce-boats alongside Staffordshire bull-baiting scenes and fruit and veg by the contemporary English potter Anne Gordon. *far right, bottom:* 1930s petal-shaped Carlton Ware in the delicious bright pastels of the day. Carlton Ware, part of Wiltshaw and Robinson, was renowned for its moulded tablewares and novelty items.

**Art Deco novelty ware**: From the 1920s, cheap and cheerful moulded botanical ceramics flourished in England. Flowers were used as raised decoration and as tableware itself – for example, waterlily, peony and buttercup plates, cups and saucers. Shorter & Sons had a good line in preserve jars disguised as strawberries, apples, pears and pineapples, and a number of Staffordshire firms turned out marmalade jars in the shape of oranges (on leaf saucers, of course) and crisp lettuce-shaped salad bowls. These delightful objects were painted brilliant green and red to represent lettuce leaves garnished with tomatoes; in another design, lobsters grasp the leaf bowl from below. The best salad ware was produced by Carlton Ware, who specialised in embossed and relief-moulded tableware; other manufacturers include John Beswick and Grimwade. Embossed novelty ware continued into the 1950s.

**Modern fruit and veg**: For the past 25 years the English potter Anne Gordon has made lively, sensitive versions of eighteenth-century porcelain fruit and vegetables. Of modern botanical ceramicists, one of the most striking is Kate Malone. Her chunky, crystalline-glazed ware includes pumpkin-shaped teapots, gourds and pineapple jugs – in 1995, for Manchester City Art Gallery, she made 'Queen Pineapple', 1.2 m (4 ft) high .

### High-relief foliage

**Palissy ware**: Bernard Palissy was an extraordinary sixteenth-century French potter (c. 1510-1590) best remembered for high-relief, sculptural pieces decorated with shells, lizards and snakes among dank, precisely delineated foliage and flowers (his sauceboat figures in baths are also great fun). To nineteenth-century French potters his work had great allure, and they revived it, especially Charles-Jean Avisseau at Tours. In England, the style was taken up by

*above:* a lead-glazed earthenware dish by Bernard Palissy, c. 1550, some of whose elements would have been modelled from life. *far right:* Palissy ware was revived in nineteenth-century France, England and Portugal; this wall of seething Palissy-style plates is in a Paris apartment; beneath it stand a trio of barbotine vases on a marble counter that was rescued from a boulangerie undergoing refurbishment. *below right:* a Minton majolica dish modelled as a white rabbit nibbling the edge of a large cabbage leaf, 1869.

*above:* moulded botanical plates gleam against painted wooden shelves. *above right:* the gelatinous green of these Wedgwood leaf plates is enhanced by their ruby background. *right:* modern asparagus dishes interspersed with Portmeirion Botanic Garden and a collection of ceramic toast racks in a medieval Shropshire farmhouse. *far right:* Bretby novelty leaf plates, with unfired ceramic biscuits stuck to them (others had moulded nuts), c.1900 ; the surround is part of a display cabinet decorated with applied dried ferns.

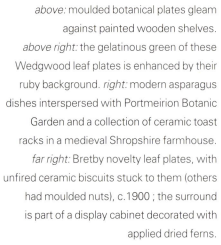

Minton. However the bulk of Palissy ware from the late nineteenth century originates from Mafra & Son in Portugal.

**Majolica**: In its predominantly green, brown and blue lead glazes, shiny, moulded majolica lends itself well to playful vegetal and animal forms (Palissy ware was a major influence). A squirrel perched on a leaf-shaped nut dish is a typical majolica object; so too is a beehive jam pot or a corncob-shaped jug. Majolica is a type of moulded earthenware covered with thick, coloured lead glazes – a far cry from the ornate tin-glaze maiolica of the Italian Renaissance. It was devised by Léon Arnoux, the French art director at Minton, and shown to acclaim at the 1851 Great Exhibition in London. Affordable and versatile, majolica objects ranged from garden ornaments to tablewares. As technology improved majolica's palette expanded to include yellow, pink and turquoise. Minton's chief rival was George Jones, while large Staffordshire makers included John Adams & Co and Wedgwood.

By the mid-1870s, its popularity in England was waning. A new market opened up in America after the 1876 Centennial Exposition in Philadelphia. The most famous American manufacturer was Griffin, Smith & Hill (later Griffin, Smith & Co) of Phoenixville, Pennsylvania. Their Shell and Seaweed wares are particularly desirable. Other major producers were Edwin Bennett of Baltimore and the Trenton Potteries, though English makers retained a special cachet. The biggest European producers were both French: Sarreguemines in Lorraine, and Onnaing. In Sweden,

*left:* 'Pineapple on Fire' – a giant pineapple jug by Kate Malone, 1996. *right:* porcelain red cabbage by Anne Gordon, who makes intricate fruit and vegetables modelled on eighteenth-century French ceramics.

Rörstrand and Gustavsberg made majolica from the late 1860s. Some American and Continental firms continued production up to the First World War.

Art potter producers of foliage include Rye Pottery, where from 1869 richly glazed brown and green jugs with applied hops and hop leaves were made, and Bretby Art Pottery in Derbyshire (founded in 1883), which fashioned cabbage-shaped jardinieres with girls peeping from the leaves, green-glazed dishes with biscuits or nuts moulded on to them, and imitation bamboo vases.

**Leaves**: In the 1750s, Derby, Longton Hall and Chelsea made their own versions of delicate Meissen vine-leaf dessert dishes. The leaves on Longton Hall's plates and sauceboats are pink-veined, turning lemon and lime-green towards the crinkly edges; often a butterfly is painted inside. Worcester's 'Blind Earl' service, made from the 1760s, possesses relief rose leaves, buds and moths. It was allegedly devised for the Earl of Coventry, who actually lost his sight in 1780.

Forests of majolica leaves appeared in the second half of the nineteenth century. Wedgwood had first made leafy ware in the late eighteenth century. After the success of majolica it revived verdant dessert plates (to several patterns, including white), which were much imitated. The glaze on relief-moulding shows darkest in the recessed parts where it is thickest – an effective, cheap and popular technique. Leaf ceramics are attractive items to collect. All look good together and there is a constant supply at reasonable prices, including modern versions. The aesthete diarist James Lees-Milne had a kitchen dresser of citrus-coloured leaf plates and the effect was spirited and spring-like. **63**

# colours & shapes

**objects collected by type or hue and displayed in pleasing patterns**

One green plate is a handsome thing. Put two on a dresser, however – even several shelves away from each other – and something happens: a theme is established, the greenness sings out and demands that the two objects are seen in relation to one another, as a composition. Plain colours are particularly good at creating such an effect, but it applies even when the unifying hue is a pattern, for example pink flowers on white crockery.

It works both with disparate and identical objects. With the latter, the eye delights in the order of massed rows: Lord Rothschild's rearrangement of Sèvres porcelain at Waddesdon – in long S's down a wall – is an unusual but memorable example of displaying a service. With disparate objects, the effect is subtler, yet it takes only a few pieces of similar shades to set up a colour leitmotif.

In collecting by shape, the same principles apply: however appealing a teacup and saucer may be, several grouped together will have more of an impact; the eye picks up the theme and revels in the rhythm and variations of form and silhouette. Shape and shade may vary considerably: if you are assembling yellow china, for example, it can range from buttercup to pale lemon and still work well together. So too a row of teapots regardless of whether all are straight-sided or one is rococo, another long and oval and a third straight-edged and hexagonal.

The fun of collecting in this way is being able to assemble pieces from different centuries and countries, of varied techniques, quality and prices and arrange them harmoniously together. This chapter is devoted to enjoyable variations on such themes.

## Colours

**Pale and interesting**: To those who espouse white walls, bleached furnishings and etiolated everything, white ceramics are obligatory – the plainer and simpler the better. However, for an object to be undecorated and still please it needs to be a particularly satisfying shape and have a fine sheen or shade of pale – happily, there are manifold degrees of whiteness, from icy bluish to rich clotted cream.

*right:* a magnificent mélange of intense hues and vase shapes ranged across a turn-of-the-century dresser by Bruce Talbot in the refulgent drawing room of the interior architect Anthony Collett; he designed the copper and forged-steel backlighters himself. The triumphant turquoise vase on top and canary-coloured ones holding onyx balls are by Bretby. The long row of ceramics are a mixture of Linthorpe and Bretby; though varied and numerous all the shapes and colours work well together.

*previous pages:* lacy rows of creamware – the cream-coloured earthenware developed by Josiah Wedgwood in the 1760s – in a collection in Bridgehampton, Long Island. The variety of shapes against the pierced plates creates a delicate overall pattern. *this page, left:* Rörstrand and Leeds creamware in the plate room at Olivehult in Sweden. Before the late eighteenth century the best tableware in a Swedish house would have been pewter; subsequently, English creamware put pewterers and faience factories out of business; Rörstrand produced quantities of creamware to compete; *right:* a collection of mostly English creamware in an eighteenth-century apothecary cabinet in a converted Maine boathouse; the walls have been painted to resemble cool limestone.

*below:* the elegant silhouette of a basalt jug, c. 1800. Black stoneware, or basalt, was perfected by Wedgwood in c. 1768, yet is still smart and modern-feeling. *right:* transfer-printed creamware plates and soup bowls, c. 1810, made at Creil in France and depicting English country houses such as Chateau de Sheffield and Chateau de Burghley. Although not a set, and of varying sizes, they make a startling composition on antique dealer Jonathan Vickers' wall, tied together by the bow and tassel.

Lovers of the blanched look need not aspire to minimalism. There is a feast of pallid china to choose from: lustrous Chinese blanc-de-chine figures, plain jelly moulds, 1930s creamware figures, and Joanna Constantinidis's snow-white porcelain cups and saucers, to pick out a few. Even cheap wares make a handsome showing, and all stand out against background colours.

The earliest white ceramic in Europe, and an attractive addition to any collection, is salt-glazed stoneware, developed in early eighteenth-century Staffordshire to emulate Chinese porcelain. Strong, bright and opaque, it could be intricately moulded; tableware was given crisp basket-work rims, rococo scrolling and pierced borders. Of the quantities of tea wares made, the most decorative was Castleford (1780-1820), picked out in blue or green. Also desirable are fantasy house and camel teapots. By 1780, the advent of creamware meant that the production of white stoneware all but ceased.

Creamware, the revolutionary eighteenth-century ceramic body, was a huge and rapid hit in Europe – and later America – after being pioneered in the mid-1760s by the great Josiah Wedgwood (1730-1795). The plain, painted and printed variety can all be found, but at a price; early shell-edged plates with tapering blue fringe are a relatively inexpensive delight. Old creamware can turn brownish, but to devotees of shabby chic this has a certain appeal. One of the best-known creamware makers, operating between 1770 and 1830, was Leeds, which specialised in high-quality thin wares and delicate pierced decoration; it has a keen following. Old creamware has been reproduced since the early nineteenth century.

Josiah Wedgwood went on perfecting creamware through the 1770s; around 1780 he introduced a whiter version with a slightly blue-tinted glaze which he called 'pearl ware'. Of similar hue was the white ironstone for which North America had a huge appetite. The original, decorated with blue and mulberry transfer-prints, was patented in England in 1813 by

Putting bright china on contrasting-coloured walls looks arresting – especially if the china is arranged in patterns. *above:* diamonds of cobalt blue plates on brilliant yellow walls in the Yorkshire kitchen of the photographer Christopher Simon Sykes. The near central ones are modern copies of eighteenth-century armorial china, surrounded by Spanish pottery. The china beyond it is eighteenth-century Chinese blue-and-white.

*right:* rows of buttery yellowware against instense blue walls in the loo of the potter Mary Wondrausch. The top plate is Greek and modern; the second row are pieces by Della Robbia of c. 1910, the third 1920s English tea ware, the fourth Italian Cantagalli of c. 1930, the fifth row consists of plates from Deruta and Moustiers, plus a tin tray; Italian, French and English 1930s vases and a jug stand on the cistern.

*right:* a parade in Long Island of American McCoy vases dating from the 1930s to the 1950s. While a single piece would look pleasant but unexceptional, ranked together the gradated colours and simple, sturdy shapes make a satisfying sequence of form and colour that draws the eye from one end of the row to the other.
*below:* green-glazed pots in a shop in L'Isle sur la Sorgue, a Provençal town famed for its copious antique shops.

A trio of unexpected colour combinations. *left:* nineteenth-century German pugs and wavy purple Ridgway plates against a ruby-red niche create a riot of warm colour and fun in this Englishwoman's dining room in Basle. The chalice is biscuitware. *below left:* nineteenth-century openwork blue plates against a singingly turquoise background create a joyous colour scheme. *right:* streaky green nineteenth-century Pilkington pots form an almost organic still life in front of lizard chairbacks designed by Anthony Collett with Nicholas Maritz.

Charles Mason; it was the embossed white-glazed kind – known as farmer's or thresher's china – that the New World cried out for from the mid-nineteenth century. It came in hundreds of patterns: tureens, pedestal dishes, jugs, teapots, jelly moulds, sauceboats, butterdishes and so on. One of the best makers was T.J. & J. Mayer.

Other pallid nineteenth-century ceramics include marble-like Parian ware and fragile, pearly Beleek from Northern Ireland, much used for shell-shaped vessels. A number of modernist designs made in white include several by the American Eva Zeisel.

**Black and white**: Some of the earliest transfer-printed wares were black designs on white (or cream) china, depicting landscapes, buildings and portraits (Creil, for example, did a series of English houses). These look smart – classical without being fusty – when displayed on a wall. In the 1950s, Pietro Fornasetti made print-like architectural teasets, which are still being reissued, and numerous other black-and-white designs.

**Black**: A powerful punctuation to coloured wares, and possessors of graceful silhouettes, black ceramics first appeared in the eighteenth century, and enjoyed a renaissance in the 1950s and 1960s in sleek, elongated coffeepots and services produced by Arabia, Wedgwood, Midwinter and others.

Unglazed basalt stoneware – so hard it could be 'polished on a lapidary wheel' – was Josiah Wedgwood's first product after silky creamware; he made large classical-style urns and vases, and some splendidly timeless coffeepots and jugs which boast precise, machine-turned or slightly raised decoration. Many Staffordshire and Continental potters made Egyptian black wares from the 1760s. The architect Sir William Chambers designed black gryphon candlesticks.

**Blue**: Not all blue wares are blue and white. For example, from the sixteenth century in Iznik pottery, both cobalt and turquoise – along with green, purple and later tawny red – were used extensively to create bright compositions of stylised tulips and other flowers. Dark blue and turquoise (*bleu celeste*) were favoured ground colours at Sèvres in the eighteenth century, and singing turquoise glazes gained favour with art potters in the nineteenth century, especially Théodore Deck and William De Morgan.

Another distinctive blue is jasper ware, Wedgwood's vitrified white stoneware stained with metallic oxides to obtain the requisite lavender shade (lilac, olive green, yellow and black were also made, but proved less popular), to which relief white decoration was applied. Jasper ware is still made and looks cool and classical.

**Yellow and green**: Since the Tang dynasty, green and yellow (from antimony) glazes have been applied to earthenware; the Romans used lead glazes from the first century AD onwards. These are soothing and attractive hues. In the eighteenth century Wedgwood and William Greatbatch both concocted green glazes, which then went out of favour until the leafy green dessert plates of the nineteenth century. The most brilliant old yellow is found in the 'canary' yellow earthenware produced in potteries in England and Wales from around 1780 to 1835 and decorated with transfer-prints or silvery lustre.

*above:* gleaming mid-nineteenth century Staffordshire silver lustreware alternated with matt-black basalt jugs in the colour-coordinated and decorative antique shop of Stephen Long in London. Most of these wares emulate Regency silver designs; the goblets on the top row would have been used as Communion cups in non-Conformist chapels.

Celadon is a softer, chalkier, semi-translucent green derived from iron, sometimes used as the only decoration on Chinese stoneware with minimal relief decorations. The first Chinese porcelain to reach England was a celadon bowl with a silver-gilt mount during the reign of Henry VIII; it is now at New College, Oxford, where it is known as 'Archbishop Warham's cup'.

Perhaps the best example of modern celadon is that produced by the British potter Edmund de Waal. He makes simple thrown porcelain shapes – a virtuoso feat as many are tall and tapering – and glazes them in a pale luscious celadon. They are pleasing contemplative pieces that work well in a group, like a monotone Morandi painting.

**Red and orange**: Possibly the richest red glazes were created during the Sung dynasty (960-1280). *Sang de boeuf* is a monochrome, mottled red – the darker patches like congealed blood – while deep *flambé* is splashed with blue or purple. Made using copper oxides, these were technically difficult to produce as they required firing at extremely high

*previous pages:* a spectacular display of Burmantofts vases against glowing gold walls in designer Anthony Collett's drawing room. Pieces are grouped by colour on the foreground dressers, as still lifes on wall brackets, and as a combination of the two on the crammed fireplace. Although modern-looking in shape and bold glazes the pots were actually produced in the late nineteenth century. *facing page:* a shimmering pink assembly of pearlware Wedgwood shell plates (*detail below*) in Palm Beach, from a dessert service introduced early in the nineteenth century.

temperatures. They were most successfully imitated in nineteenth-century France and England. The British potter Rupert Spira has recently made a range using 'Sung' glazes.

During the jazz-age 1920s, raging oranges came into their own on ceramics – for example those by Clarice Cliff. Over the next few decades kitchen and workaday American ceramics such as Hall China Company's refrigerator wares regularly used post-box reds and other hot hues. More recent smart monochromes include the daisy-shaped plates made by Maryse Boxer.

**Redware and terracotta**: Unglazed red stoneware was first made at Yixing from the late Ming period. This was imitated in Japan, by the Elers brothers in Staffordshire in the late seventeenth century, by Böttger at Meissen (just before porcelain was evolved) and elsewhere. Fired at a high temperature, it was quite unlike low-fired terracotta. In the late nineteenth century Christopher Dresser made terracotta designs for the Watcombe Terracotta Co. Julian Stair fashions contemporary red stoneware pieces.

**Lustre**: The first European ceramics to use iridescent, metallic-painted decoration were twelfth-century Hispano-Moresque wares. Of the rest of Europe, only England produced lustreware in any quantity, and only from the late eighteenth century. Naive pink-lustre patterns and landscapes were splashily drawn on white tea wares. Their unpretentious depiction and glinting pink still look decorative in a modern setting.

Lustre comes in three forms: silver (derived from platinum, and first discovered in 1750), bronze, copper and gold (all from gold), and pink, made from a gold powder known as Purple of Cassius. It can be applied in three ways: all over, on top of a sugary or wax 'resist' so that the lustre sticks to the unpainted sections, or as a painted decoration.

*left:* a pretty-pink 'London'-shaped porcelain tea service of c. 1815 forms a lustrous cluster on, above and below contrastingly cream and baby-blue hanging shelves; on the table is a Staffordshire lustre pearlware bough pot also of 1815, plus a small 'moonlight' lustre pot; naively painted lustreware was produced in great quantities in England from the early nineteenth century. *right:* trompe l'oeil *fond bois* porcelain behind wire and framed by a lustrous wood display case; it was a popular genre that originated at Niderviller c. 1770, and was imitated by most Continental factories.

*above:* an extremely elegant white ceramic vessel by Diego Giacometti in the St Jean Cap Ferrat home of couturier Hubert Givenchy. Just one such object commands attention by its stateliness alone.

At first silver lustre was applied chiefly to rims and for detailing. From 1840 to 1870, before electro-plating allowed imitation silverware, it was used on white wares to create 'poor man's silver'. From 1950 to 1980 Royal Worcester made gold and silver tea and coffee services. Today, metallic-painted tableware is made in Eastern Europe.

Nineteenth-century lustreware was produced in greatest quantity in Staffordshire and in Sunderland, which is associated with sponged-on 'splash-lustre' – what Wedgwood called 'moonlight' or 'Holy door marble'. Lustre was also used to spice up jugs commemorating political events and the openings of railways or bridges, and on hanging-plaques containing ships or mottoes. Very little lustreware of this period is marked. In the early twentieth century lustre was revived, particularly at Gray's Pottery (for example, Gloria Lustre). In recent years potters such as Alan Caiger-Smith have used it; Brenda Taylor creates pink lustre and shell dinner services, while the South African potter Hylton Nel has put versions of nineteenth-century pink-lustre houses on earthenware mugs.

## Shapes

The tilt of a jug's lip, the long neck of a vase and the arching handle of a teapot are some of the elements that determine whether a ceramic object is plain dull or thrillingly attractive. Quite apart from aesthetics, they also announce its history: a bullet-shaped teapot, for example, is likely to date from the 1750s; a simple, green-ridged 1930s vase may well be by Keith Murray at Wedgwood. Domestic tableware comes in dramatically different guises, even over the space of a decade. The frilly and ornate may not match the straight-edged and austere – indeed, each will attract different collectors – but both look striking when arranged with other similar objects.

Grouping pieces by subject works well, whether flocks of china sheep, bright cottage-shaped pastille burners or long, lanky sauce-boats paraded lip to handle like waddling ducks. The fun comes in part from the mix – black basalt coffeepots alongside Wemyss-ware jam pots; cow creamers with creamware; a row of elongated 1930s Constance Spry plant holders interspersed with dendritic mochaware jugs.

The shapes of domestic pottery over the past 300-odd years have been strongly influenced by fine metalware. Indeed, during the eighteenth century, it was possible to tell silver tableware fashions from the ceramic milk jugs and coffeepots that mimicked them. The soaring popularity of tea around the time porcelain was invented – the early eighteenth century – led to two new European pottery shapes: a teapot for brewing leaves in and tea bowls adapted from Chinese originals, on saucers. While tea bowls – and teacups from 1780 – were always made from china, teapots were often fashioned in rococo silver, later translated into clay. Other items commonly based on silverware were sauce-boats, tureens and sugar bowls.

**Teapots**: There is something comically appealing about the teapot, with its spout one end and handle the other. It lends itself admirably to fanciful forms, from monkeys to cauliflowers, cottages and cars. A number of extensive, entertaining and elegant collections of teapots are open to the public. Collectors can make their selection by picking on differences or similarities in shape, types of decoration, factory or period.

**Jugs**: Myriad types of this apparently simple vessel exist: water jugs, helmet jugs, ewers with basins, milk jugs, cream jugs, wine jugs, toby jugs, even puzzle jugs with a confusing proliferation of spouts. They come in all ceramic types and shapes that range from conical to globular, ovoid, helmet-shaped, tall, and long and low, like sauce-boats.

A widely made mid-nineteenth-century English ceramic was the relief-moulded stoneware jug, designed to keep drinks cool. Unglazed and inexpensive to make, they were turned out in great number by Ridgway & Abington, Doulton, Charles Meigh and Minton, among others. Most have a maker's name. Sometimes off-white and sometimes dyed a variety of shades, they were decorated with relief elements such as twisting convolvulus or vine motifs, saints in niches, ears of corn or bacchanalian orgies, and look fabulous *en masse*.

**Coffee cups and teacups**: Collecting single teacups, coffee cups and cans – with or without saucers – is inexpensive and entertaining. They are often exquisitely painted

*previous pages, left:* a collection of early nineteenth-century Castleford teapots in moulded stoneware with characteristic smart coloured edges, their spouts aloft and facing inwards to create a balanced composition; *right:* assorted teacups pleasingly assembled on a grid-like shelf in Williamstown, Massachusetts. *this page, above:* an array of mid-nineteenth century relief-moulded jugs by various Staffordshire manufacturers. The central one commemorates the death of Prince Albert and its handle is made up of his many honours. The peacock wall plates are by John Pearson and the stoneware water filter is Doulton; *right:* plain nineteenth-century stoneware jelly moulds, designed for practical use but gloriously decorative in this kitchen line-up at Tredegar House, Newport.

and do not need to match in colour or be of similar period in order to look good together. Being relatively small, a number can fit into even a restricted space.

Tea wares used to be very small in their earliest European incarnation, reflecting the high cost of tea. Teacups, rather than bowls, were first made at Sèvres, after the Seven Years' War (1756-63), and the straight-sided coffee cup followed in the 1780s and 1790s. Both tea and coffee cups were designed to be useful and decorative – only fashionable people drank tea and coffee, a fact which elegant drinking vessels reflected.

**Kitchenware**: Many of the most unusual and inexpensive intriguingly shaped wares are once-practical and now obsolete objects such as oval meat platters, which contain a number of holes originally designed to let the meat's juices run through. Their simple abstract shape is seen to good advantage on a wall. Similarly, decorative lids of long-broken casseroles can be effectively displayed on tablescape or wall. Drug or apothecary jars, originally used for storing herbs or medicines in pharmacies around Europe from the sixteenth century onwards, come in pleasing sets with lettering describing their – often toxic – contents. Attractive reproductions have been made in the last hundred years, for example, in the 1920s Basil Ionides designed a set for Culpeper, the herbalists, who still make small culinary ones.

Jelly moulds are simple three-dimensional sculptures. Josiah Wedgwood introduced creamware ones big enough for several helpings in the 1770s – until then they were designed for individual portions only. The Wedgwood moulds consisted of decorated inner and plain, fluted outer moulds. The painted inner pyramid stayed inside the jelly to support and enhance it – the patterns showing through. From the 1840s, thick, cheap stoneware moulds appeared; these are the ones the collector is most likely to come across, and though they are no longer inexpensive, a few displayed together make a satisfying decoration.

# rustic

**slipware, spongeware and other country crocks**

The more urban and mechanised our lives become, the more we yearn for the simplicity of a traditional rural way of life – or at least a prettified version of it, without any of the discomfort of the real thing. However, one of the rustic household's most delightful manifestations is also one of its most practical, namely unpretentious hand-made earthenware – the mainstay of cottage potteries to the end of the eighteenth century, and still made on a small scale today.

Rustic pottery's shiny glazes, bold decoration and solid simple shapes translate delightfully into modern metropolitan life. Fired at low temperatures and designed for daily use, it is often chipped or distressed, which adds to its charm. It is chunky rather than delicate, made by hand and therefore slightly irregular – each piece different – while the basic utilitarian shapes have remained unchanged over many decades. In Europe, America and beyond, the country pottery provided surrounding villages with plain or simply adorned kitchen and tableware – often naive versions of grander ceramics. Before the advent of refrigerators, earthenware pitchers and jars were used to store and keep cool all manner of fresh, dried and pickled foods and liquids ranging from milk to cider to oil.

**Decline and revival of country potteries**

By the turn of the nineteenth century in Western Europe and North America, the introduction of cheaper faience, tough-wearing

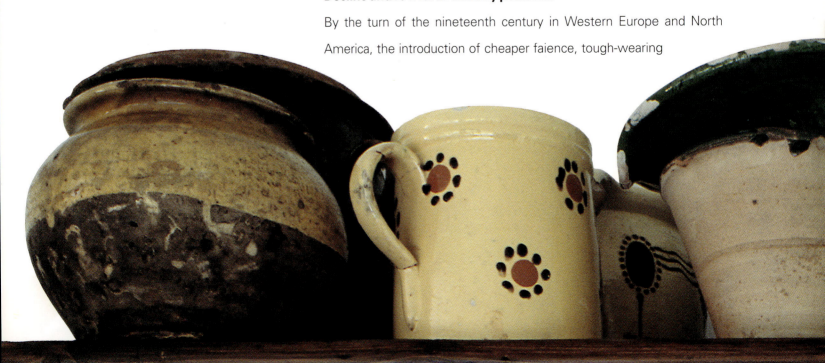

creamware and transfer ware had caused local potteries to decline. A century on, the disappearance of most of the rest (about 100 in Britain) was hastened by the shortage of manpower in the First World War and the arrival of gas cookers, refrigerators and new storage materials such as Pyrex and plastic. From then on, aesthetic appeal governed the survival of rustic wares. In the 1920s and 1930s, rural crafts enjoyed a revival as the middle classes started to patronise local potteries and to import rustic ware from France, Italy and Czechoslovakia. Individual potters such as Bernard Leach and Michael Cardew began to relearn and practise traditional potting techniques.

More recently, extensive travel has introduced people to rustic ceramic traditions world-wide, and kept them going. Every country has its own 'primitive' domestic ware. Throughout Europe, the flat, simplified representation of leaves and other motifs is extremely similar, while slip and sgraffito techniques are universal. To see old vernacular wares, visit local museums. For purchasers, pre-nineteenth-century pieces are prohibitively expensive, but nineteenth- and twentieth-century kitchenware is reasonable, serviceable, and often identical to earlier pieces. In peasant cultures outside Western Europe and North America, for example parts of Romania and Mexico, strong local pottery-making traditions endure. The term 'rustic' in this chapter applies to rough crocks, more sophisticated country techniques, and exuberantly painted folk pottery.

*below:* a cluster of crude, part-painted Provençal earthenware pots – of a type used for centuries in Mediterranean countries to carry or store water, wine, oil and other foodstuffs. The slippery lead glaze is often pleasingly distressed – fired at low temperatures it flakes easily; the glaze is most commonly green – from copper oxide; impurities in the lead glaze turn it a rich yellow colour.

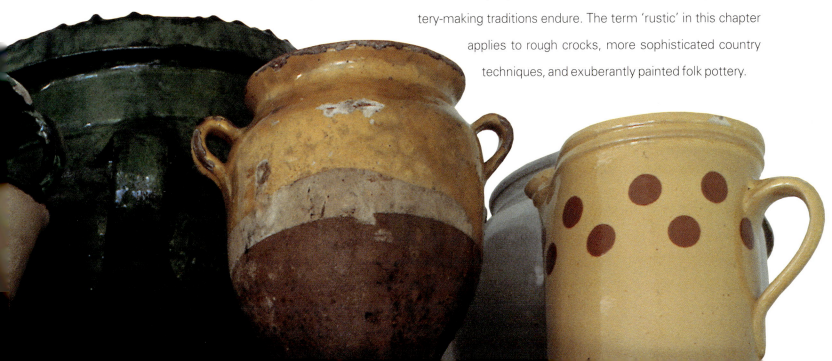

**Decorating with rustic pottery**

Rustic pottery, with its overtones of the pastoral idyll, looks attractive and homely in a kitchen – even a modern one. A few pieces on a dresser transport the observer to the Mediterranean – in the case of yellow or green glazed ware – or to the jolliest dirndl-wearing part of Eastern Europe where folk-painted flowers are concerned. For lovers of a sombre palette, there is a large supply of brown jars, dishes and bowls – many part-terracotta, part-glazed – to choose from. (Lead glazes, poisonous for potters and con-sumers alike, were largely discontinued by the mid-twentieth century; there is no fully adequate substitute for their slippery sheen.) Lack of decoration is reflected in low prices.

Only a few authentic country potteries still operate in Britain. Brannam's in Barnstaple and Aller Vale in South Devon were both art potteries in the late nineteenth century be-fore reverting to traditional pitchers, planters, casseroles, bread crocks and flowerpots; Wetheriggs in Cumbria makes traditional slipwares; while George Curtis at Ripon, Yorkshire produces strawberry and garden pots.

**Slipware**

One of the most attractive forms of folk pottery is slipware: lead-glazed earthenware decorated with dots, lines and zigzags of coloured slip (clay mixed with water to the consistency of cream), and fired. It is an ancient way of decorating pottery, practised in China, Ancient Greece and the Byzantine world long before reaching Western Europe.

**British slipware**: The Romans made slipware in Britain, but the oldest complete pieces (sixteenth to eighteenth century) come from Wrotham in Kent: huge dark-bodied platters, loving cups and candlesticks painted with lighter slip in the same way as a cake might be iced. Other slipware items include tygs (drinking cups), miniature pottery cradles given as fertility symbols to young married couples, and possets for drinking hot milk curdled with ale or spiced wine.

Slipware had blossomed into an 'art' form by the seventeenth century, thanks to a fami-ly of Staffordshire potters, the Tofts, who made splendid ornamental circular dishes.

*previous pages:* this corner of a country
cottage houses the potter Mary Wondrausch's
study collection of nineteenth- and early
twentieth-century European slipwares. The
large reddish plate on the top row of the Irish
fiddleback dresser is a Yorkshire baking dish of
1870-1900. *this page, left:* a chorus of C.H.
Brannam milk pitchers – Brannam's in Devon is
one of Britain's few surviving traditional country
potteries – in Mary Wondrausch's kitchen; on
the table are slipware plates and soup bowls by
her; *above:* late nineteenth-century Verwood
jugs and Sussex and Cornwall pitchers on
another window sill in the same room.

Typically, these contain a fanciful drawing in dark brown slip, outlined with white dots and filled in with reddish slip, all under a yellow glaze. On the rim is a two-tone trellis border inset with a name (often a signature). The Tofts' subjects are mostly royal portraits or mythic creatures such as a mermaid. All combine charm and a bold naivety. The Toft style was prevalent for around 80 years. Smaller objects were commissioned to mark weddings and christenings, a tradition revived by the contemporary English slipware-maker Mary Wondrausch.

The Toft drawing method is known as trailing: a design is 'trailed' on to an object through a narrow tube (originally a quill) using different coloured slips. Other slipware techniques include combing (or feathering), marbling, sprigging and sgraffito. In combing, lines of trailed slip are applied and 'combed' by drawing a bristle or stripped feather across them, to create a pleasing regular pattern. Marbling involves adding lines of slip to a coat of another colour, and jiggling the object about to swirl the slips together; it is often combined with combing. In sprigging, separately moulded pieces are attached to an object. A rarer technique, found especially in eighteenth-century Devon around Bideford, is sgraffito, which involves carving or scratching a design through a layer of slip to expose the darker body below.

By the late eighteenth century slipware seemed old-fashioned in the face of imported Chinese porcelain and cheap creamware. None the less certain types continued to be made. For instance, sgraffito jugs celebrating the harvest and sheep-shearing were made till the late nineteenth century. Motifs include birds, smartly dressed ladies with scythes, ears of corn, ships and poems on the joys of drinking cider. In the late nineteenth century, the South Devon potteries around Torquay – Watcombe, Royal Torquay

and Aller Vale – produced souvenir sgraffito objects, from teapots to hair curler rests. Edwin Beer Fishley, whom Bernard Leach termed 'the last vital peasant potter in England', made sgraffito jugs at his Fremington pottery in Devon from 1860 to 1912 which inspired Michael Cardew as a child. Sgraffito ware was also made in nineteenth-century Pennsylvania, at Beauvais, and in southern France up to the 1960s.

In England, traditional slipware techniques had fallen into abeyance by the early 1900s when Reginald Wells (1877-1951) set up a pottery in Wrotham and began to make slip-wares similar to Wrotham ware. More influentially, in St Ives in the 1920s, Bernard Leach (1887-1979) and – until 1923 when he returned to Japan – the Japanese potter Shoji Hamada (1894-1978) revived slipware techniques.

Michael Cardew (1901-1983), Leach's next pupil, was a lifelong promoter of traditional domestic ware. After three years with Leach he set up on his own at Winchcombe in Gloucestershire and re-opened the old farmhouse pottery. His sturdy slipware boasts luscious glazes from honey yellow to treacly brown, decorated with vigorous, yet elegant lines. Cardew sold functional items at low prices, believing that potters should make 'domestic, useful, usable pottery . . . things you can eat and drink from, in considerable quantities'. He later moved to Wenford Bridge, in Cornwall, leaving Winchcombe in the hands of Ray Finch (born 1914) who has made tableware there ever since. His son Seth Cardew (born 1934) continues to work at Wenford Bridge.

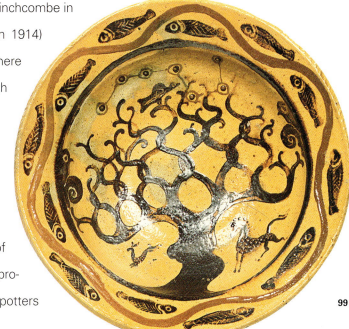

After the Second World War, Bernard Leach influenced a wide-scale re-emergence of small 'brown mug' potteries producing domestic ware. Many potters

*facing page:* this Staffordshire coronation charger signed 'William Talor', 1675, probably portrayed the coronation of Charles II in 1661; it was designed purely for decoration and display, and identified its owner as a royalist. *above:* contemporary slipware dish by Mary Wondrausch. *below right:* Bernard Leach revived slipware in the 1920s; this plate showing the Tree of Life is dated 1923.

*right:* Mary Wondrausch's collection of Thun ware, the most elaborate slipware in Europe, which was bought as souvenirs by nineteenth-century tourists on walking holidays in Switzerland; there are still some 30 potteries around Lake Thun. In England, South Devon motto ware fulfilled the same function, only for the working classes. The fire surround was built by Wondrausch's son Hugo and painted by her. *below:* detail of a Swiss terracotta dish, c. 1920.

*left*: the rich chestnut shades of American
redware in this log cabin-cum-studio in Warren
County, New Jersey create a warm ruddy
ambience. *above:* spotted French and
American lead-glazed earthenwares sit happily
together in a dresser in rural Connecticut.

*below:* modernistic round teapot (1995) in salt-glazed stoneware by Walter Keeler, the man who revived the genre in England in the 1970s. *right:* nineteenth-century American stoneware in a period setting at Deerfield, Massachusetts, where a number of old houses form a 'living museum'. The best-known New England stoneware, usually salt-glazed and often slip-trailed with cobalt, was produced by the Norton Pottery in Bennington, Vermont.

were trained by Leach, others by Cardew and Finch; most plumped for hard-wearing stoneware, with a few using earthenware. Among the best-known creators of 'rustic-looking' pots, are Richard Batterham (born 1936), Henry Hammond (1914-1989), Michael Casson (born 1925), Harry Davis (1910-1986), John Leach (born 1939; Bernard Leach's grandson), Jim Malone and Svend Bayer (born 1946). Thoroughly modern slipware was made by Sam Haile (1909-1948) and his wife Marianne de Trey (born 1913) at Dartington. Recently slipware has been revived by such potters as David Garland (born 1941), Clive Bowen (born 1943) and Geoffrey Fuller (born 1936).

**Salt-glazing**: Another sturdy European pottery technique is stoneware glazed with salt – which is thrown into a burningly hot kiln, creating an 'orange peel' surface. The technique was brought to Britain from Germany in the seventeenth century, and used for tankards, jugs and, later on, Cooper's marmalade jars and even hot-water bottles. It was revived in the 1970s by Walter Keeler (born 1942), who at first made functional thrown pieces and later more exaggerated, modern shapes.

### Continental slipware and American redware

Beauvais was the centre of slipware in France from the early seventeenth century. However the most impressive European slipwares from the sixteenth century onwards came from Germany. Today, traditional slipware is still made in Alsace Lorraine – chestnut-brown cooking ware trailed with white, green and orange flowers and leaves – and at Grenzhausen in the Westerwald. In Spain, some potteries in Galicia still use lead glazes for slipware; as do others in Sicily.

Colonial America was fertile ground for plain domestic pottery, including redware, yellowware and ironware. Redware was the first. From the late seventeenth century, while tableware was mostly imported from the Old World, pitchers, platters and storage jars were fashioned locally to European styles using the plentiful red clay, and decorated in simplified slipware style. The

technique seems to have been brought over from Germany and Switzerland. Plates were sometimes used for a primitive kind of advertising, with a tavern's name, or dishes such as 'lemon pie' or 'clams & oysters' scrawled in slip. Redware's shapes and decorations remained unchanged until the late nineteenth century when it was supplanted by other ceramics.

## Rural French potteries

Provence has for centuries been home to a plethora of country potteries, some of which survive to this day, making predominantly green, yellow and reddish-brown wares, with painted, splashed or stamped decoration. In the village of Pöet Laval, near Dieulefit, for example, techniques little used since the early twentieth century have been revived by Jacques Robin. His traditional tableware is first moulded, fashioned further on a wheel, dried in the sun, dipped in a glaze and fired; a wood-powered kiln was used until 1990. Many forms are based on old silver: octagonal plates with beaded rims, and 'Louis XV' plates with a dark brown line round the rim.

Other long-established Provençal pottery centres include Uzès and Apt, which both have traditions of 'marbled' or agateware china. In Apt, where clay occurs in myriad different colours, just one potter, Jean Faucon, continues the technique, using inherited plaster moulds of eighteenth-century shapes. Biot, Aubagne and Anduze all produce garden pots. The most famous are those of Anduze, devised in the seventeenth century by a family of potters named Boisset, and inspired by Italian Medici vases. Their swagged, deep-eggcup shapes have green splashes on an ochre-coloured glaze. They were designed for outdoor use – a novel idea at the time. The architect François Mansart planted them with orange trees and placed them in the gardens at Versailles. Several potters produce Anduze vases; there is a long waiting list for those by the Boisset descendants.

The most famous South of France pottery town is Vallauris, which even in the nineteenth century shipped quantities of cooking ware round the

Motifs on rustic ware tend to endure. *below left:* eighteenth-century American redware bowl. *right:* earthenware bird charger by Michael Cardew, c. 1930, an example of what Bernard Leach called 'the most genuine lead-glazed slipware since the eighteenth century'. To fill his vast kiln at Winchcombe Pottery in Gloucestershire (1926-39), Cardew often made 350 to 500 pots a month, and decorated them himself.

Mediterranean. After the Second World War it became famous for its art pottery – thanks to Picasso's inventive pieces, made at the Madoura Pottery.

The most renowned naive hand-painted French earthenware is produced by Quimper, in Britanny. Characteristic designs in yellow, blue, orange and green depict people in Breton dress, with a feathery rim pattern; other potteries have used similar designs. The factory at Loc Maria, near Quimper, was founded in the late seventeenth century; within 50 years chinoiserie and rococo decorations appeared there. By the 1870s Quimper had started to produce versions of its eighteenth-century wares. These are still made today: typical motifs include flowers and leaves framing a bird, ship or house.

## East European folk ware

Europe's brightest and jolliest folk pottery is found in Eastern Europe, where rural life has changed comparatively little over the past century. In parts of Slovakia, Bratislava and Transylvania, for example, decorative pottery was and is a house's chief adornment, and jaunty painted plates are traditionally hung on the wall like paintings. Most East European pottery shares similar forms and decorations – for example, lipless wine jugs, large water jugs, and cheerful flower, animal and bird motifs. Such pieces are rarely found in Western Europe, but may be obtained cheaply in their countries of origin.

## Yellowware

In the nineteenth century, every kitchen in North America would have contained yellowware mixing bowls. Plain, utilitarian, and heat resistant, yellowware was another cheap ceramic named after the clay it was made from. Though developed in Britain – particularly Derbyshire and Yorkshire – it is found mostly in the US, where it was made

*previous pages:* traditional brightly painted folk ware plasters the walls of these houses in the Muramures region of north-west Romania. *this page:* nineteenth-century Quimper and more basic rustic crocks displayed in smartly contrasting plate racks in kitchens in Brittany; at far right spoons are held up by the racks – just as forks are on the previous page.

from the early nineteenth century. A cottage industry grew up in New Jersey, Kentucky, Pennsylvania and New England, and turned large-scale after the introduction of gas-fired kilns in the 1870s.

Early bowls were plain, but surface decoration – ribbing, moulding, even embossing – crept in, as did coloured bands and sponging. Yellow glazes from pale primrose to deep mustard were the most popular, but green and tortoiseshell spatter glazes (Rockingham ware) can also be found. The main centre of manufacture was East Liverpool, Ohio; yellowware continued to be made in the Midwest into the 1930s.

### Spongeware

Another domestic nineteenth-century ceramic with rustic associations is spongeware. Made from white Staffordshire ironstone or pearlware, it was named after the sponges used to dab decoration on to it, which ranged from abstract patterns to simple motifs applied with cut sponges – or sometimes, in Scotland and Ireland, with potato stamps or

bits of cloth. Blue was the favourite colour, but dark pink, green, brown, grey and yellow spongeware was also made. The almost insatiable American demand was mostly supplied by England.

Spongeware's ancestor is the mottled yellow-brown-and-green glaze perfected in the 1740s by the master potter Thomas Whieldon (1719-1795). A decade on, Whieldon teamed up with the young Josiah Wedgwood. Together they experimented with glazes, and created effects that mimicked agate, marble and tortoiseshell – later much imitated. Over the next century England exported quantities of sponge and spatter ware (decoration applied with a brush) to the Americas, the Far East and West Africa. In the 1860s, one producer alone, W. Adams & Co of Stoke, made 70,000 dozen pieces a week for foreign markets.

Spongeware techniques were also exported, to French ceramic centres such as Forges-les-Eaux, Sarreguemines and Lunéville. They later caught on in The

*left:* an impressive assembly of antique blue-and-white spongeware in the Connecticut farmhouse of Susan and Jerry Lauren; the three rows of nothing but jugs are pleasing variations on a theme. Despite the fact that spongeware was a popular utilitarian ceramic, and thus likely to be damaged through use, the Laurens allow no cracks or chips; all their pieces are perfect.

*above:* a wall of antique kitchenware separates the kitchen and living room in Suzanne Slesin's East Coast American home. She picked up the yellowware bowls and other china in fleamarkets.

*above:* an early mochaware jug of c. 1830-40, with typical 'tree-like' markings. *right:* a cool, contemporary rustic sill in an attic bathroom in the Malvern Hills. The stoneware jug by Walter Keeler sits comfortably with the other textures: a 'seed pod' wooden bowl by Jim Partridge, a stone bowl, and a basket by Jenny Crisp.

Netherlands, Germany, Belgium and Portugal. By the end of the nineteenth century the US had become a major producer, at Red Wing, Minnesota; East Liverpool, Ohio; Maryland and Trenton, New Jersey, where sponging was also applied to stoneware and yellowware. In Europe plates and bowls often had sponged borders around motifs such as roosters.

Spongeware fell out of fashion after the First World War, and has only been successfully revived in the last few decades; in England by Emma Bridgewater, Brixton Pottery and others. In spite of the amount of spongeware made, old pieces are comparatively rare; slightly damaged ones are well worth considering.

## Mochaware

Mochaware is a cheap, thick white china distinguished by branching tree-like designs on a coloured band. It was chiefly made in England from the late eighteenth century in the form of beer mugs and jugs for pubs and kitchens. Shards of it have been found in the slave quarters at Monticello, the home of the eighteenth-century American president Thomas Jefferson.

It was named after the dendritic markings in cut moss agate or mocha stone from Mocha in Arabia (modernday Yemen). Similar patterns were created on ceramic by dripping a few drops of secret 'tea' on to a wide band of usually blue, grey or mustard slip. Tea was a mixture of tobacco juice, urine, turpentine and other substances, which reacted with the damp slip and spread into a dark frond-like 'silhouette' of a tree in winter.

Staffordshire and Yorkshire were the centres of nineteenth-century mochaware production; it was also made by Leeds Pottery, Edge and Malkin in Burslem and T.G. Green of Derbyshire (who briefly revived it in the 1980s). Charles Dickens witnessed its manufacture at Spode in Stoke-on-Trent in 1852 and described the process. Many pieces – most unmarked – were exported to America; France also manufactured mochaware in quantity. It has a sturdy charm and is still relatively inexpensive.

# figures & animals

**a crew of china companions, from birds to beasts to theatrical beings**

There is something endearingly friendly about peopling a home with representations of man and beast. A china figure has a real presence in a room: exotic, playful or pretty as gesture and painted features allow, supplying a focus to ledge or wall, breathing life into moribund corners, sitting in cheerful isolation in a niche.

The desire for china companions goes back a long way: in ancient China, people of note were buried with a pottery entourage of up-to-life-size figures and animals, so as to recreate in the after-world their circumstances in life. (The recent influx of Han, Tang and Ming tomb figures into Europe has rendered them far more available and affordable than ever before.) This chapter charts the development of human and animal china in Europe from fanciful eighteenth-century porcelain to cruder jaunty Staffordshire pottery of the Victorian era and sleek Art Deco creamware.

### Eighteenth-century figures

Some of the earliest European porcelain images were small Chinese buddhas made from the 1720s at Meissen, Saint-Cloud and Chantilly. Early Meissen figures also aped the creations of court confectioners, whose elaborate allegorical characters in wax, sugar or confectioner's gum had since medieval times been displayed at the dessert stage of banquets. The new wonder material of porcelain could be modelled more intricately, with a greater sense of movement, a magnificent sheen and sharp, fresh colours. By the 1750s porcelain table decorations were the rage across Europe. In 1753 Horace Walpole (1717-1797) wrote in 'The World': 'Jellies, biscuits, sugar-plumbs, and creams have long given way to harlequins, gondoliers, Turks, Chinese, and shepherdesses of Saxon china . . . By degrees, whole meadows of cattle, of the same brittle materials, spread themselves over the whole table . . . pigmy Neptunes in cars of cockle-shells triumphed over oceans of looking-glass or seas of silver tissue . . . Confectioners found their trade moulder away, while toymen and china-shops were the only fashionable purveyors of the last stage of polite entertainments.' Few pottery figures were made in Europe before the eighteenth century. That exquisite porcelain statues should be treated as objects of wonder – the table a stage to strut on amid a riot of sweetmeats – seems entirely appropriate. Meissen and other new porcelain factories enjoyed a preponderance of theatrical themes, in particular from the Commedia dell'Arte.

### Meissen

Augustus the Strong, Elector of Saxony (1670-1733), had a grand passion for porcelain. He founded Meissen in 1710 and when in 1721 he started to build a Japanese Palace in Dresden, he commissioned a series of monumental birds and animals for it, with Johann Gottlob Kirchner in charge. No one had fired this size of porcelain before, and numerous problems arose. Then, in 1731, Augustus found a new recruit, Johann Joachim Kändler (1706-1775), pupil to the court sculptor.

Kändler had an extraordinary facility for fashioning porcelain. He made sketches at Moritzburg zoo (earlier animals had been modelled from prints), from which 70 lively, naturalistic porcelain creatures were made, some over a metre high. They include a parrot about to take flight, bears, and a life-size heron with a frog on its base. The Victoria and Albert Museum in London has examples of these spectacular white creatures, and there are many more at the Zwinger Palace in Dresden. The project came to an end after Augustus's death, but Kändler's style endured. He was chief modeller at Meissen from 1733 to 1775, and his vast output com-

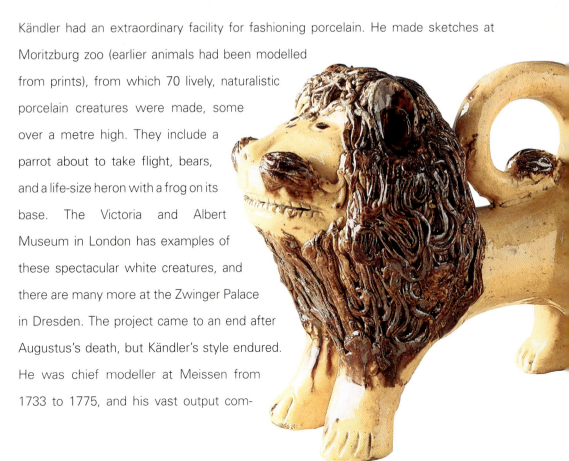

*left:* a gorgeously painted Bow porcelain figure representing Autumn, c. 1765-70, from a set of the Seasons at Fenton House in London; it is typical of the rococo figures produced by English factories in the second half of eighteenth century, imitating earlier German ones but even more elaborate. *right:* an earthenware lion, made 1840-65 in Waynesboro, Pennsylvania by John Bell, one of three potting brothers in the Shenandoah Valley. They created whimsical, naive animals as toys or doorstops; John also copied Staffordshire spaniels.

*right:* some of the large white animals made 1728-1730 by Johann Gottlob Kirchner at Meissen for Augustus the Strong's porcelain menagerie and now at the Zwinger Palace in Dresden. As the biggest porcelain objects ever attempted they were a technical feat and far from perfect. Kirchner worked from prints of animals, so his models are stylised rather than lifelike; he was joined in 1731 by the young Johann Joachim Kändler, who by contrastcreated naturalistic birds and animals from life (*above*, a tern, c. 1740); Augustus the Strong was so impressed that he replaced Kirchner with Kändler, who went on to revolutionise the way man and beast were represented in china. Kändler was chief modeller at Meissen from 1733 to 1775.

prised more than 1,000 figures and animals – from prints as well as from life. Among his assistants were Johann Friedrich Eberlein (1693-1749) and Peter Reinicke (1715-1768).

After the monumental animals Kändler began to fashion small figures (12.5-20cm/5-8in) which, being table settings, needed to look good in the round. His Harlequins, Columbines and Pantaloons of the 1730s and 1740s swagger animatedly, their exaggerated gestures heightened by black, red, green and yellow costumes, their twisted poses giving the illusion of movement from every angle. Also popular were fashionably dressed courtiers and exotic subjects (the French painter François Boucher was a favourite source), while more unexpected characters include miners and beggars. Meissen figures were exported throughout Europe, copied by the new factories that sprang up, and by 1749 were for sale at Ranelagh Pleasure Gardens in London.

In 1756, the Seven Years' War broke out and Meissen's production halted. When it resumed in the 1760s, a more restrained neo-classical style was attempted under Michel-Victor Acier (1736-1795). Figures received plainer modelling and backs were left unpainted – for display in cabinets. In the nineteenth century, many Meissen figures harked back to the rococo designs of the first half of the eighteenth century .

Meissen figures are not necessarily beyond the collector's purse. In the 1970s a warder in the Porcelain Galleries at the Victoria and Albert Museum in London decided to collect Meissen figures himself. At first he bought inferior nineteenth-century pieces. Then, as his interest and expertise grew, he began to focus on the best eighteenth-century figures. The extent and quality of his collection was revealed only when he gave it to the museum.

### Other eighteenth-century porcelain figures

Kändler's closest rival was Franz Anton Bustelli (1723-1763), Nymphenburg's chief modeller from 1754 until his death. Many of his delicate and coquettish putti, lovers among ruins and Commedia dell'Arte figures are still made today. Other notable European modellers include Etienne-Maurice Falconet (1716-1791) at Sèvres, whose unglazed 'biscuit' figures were copied throughout Europe; and Johann Peter Melchior

*left:* dancing eighteenth-century English figures in a painted dresser; above them sit magnificent Chelsea sunflower plates and other botanical delights. *below:* a Meissen Commedia dell'Arte Harlequin of 1733 by Johann Joachim Kändler. Its typically twisting *contrapposto* ensures that the figure's movement is visible from all angles; it can be seen at Fenton House in London, a National Trust property.

*above:* an early nineteenth-century English figure of a gardener, set amongst leafy bocage. Bocage was first used in eighteenth-century England – unlike hard-paste German porcelain figures, soft-paste English ones tended to collapse without support. *below right:* bocage sheep and deer of c. 1820 march along the top of a hanging shelf. The best-known makers of animals with bocage were Ralph Wood, his son, also Ralph Wood, and John Walton.

(1742-1825), who specialised in rosy-cheeked children and biscuit portrait reliefs at Hochst, Frankenthal and Nymphenburg. At Capodimonte, near Naples, Giuseppe Gricci (1700-1770) made gentle soft-paste religious subjects, hawkers and fishermen.

Many eighteenth-century English figures, at Chelsea, Bow and Derby, were adapted from hard-paste Meissen or Sèvres – Meissen even lent examples to the British Ambassador to Saxony for Chelsea to copy – though temperamental English soft-paste often required leafy bocage support to keep its shape. Most figures came in pairs or sets such as the Four Seasons or the Continents, and classical subjects abounded. In contrast with Meissen, English figures became increasingly elaborate until the 1770s. However, they are more plentiful and therefore less expensive than Meissen.

### Eighteenth- and early nineteenth-century animals

Pre-eighteenth-century European animal pottery tends to be somewhat drab: slipware owl jugs (much faked) and English and German salt-glazed bear-jars with removable heads for cups and shredded clay for fur. By contrast, porcelain Chinese export animals and birds – dogs, monkeys, cranes – shipped to Europe from the seventeenth century onwards, were exotic and brightly coloured.

As with figures, an explosion in ceramic creatures occurred hard on the heels of the European discovery of porcelain around 1709. At Meissen, Kändler made a stream of animals, which were imitated throughout Europe. Among the most popular were dogs, in particular pugs. Tureens in the shape of hens, turkeys, swans, rabbits and boars' heads appeared in porcelain at Meissen and Chelsea, and in faience at Strasbourg, Marseilles and Sceaux; the Chinese imitated them too. In England, animal-head stirrup cups were made. More startling was the *Affenkappelle*, or Monkey Band (1753-55) by Kändler and Reinicke, of monkeys in human finery playing musical instruments; it was copied at Chelsea and other factories.

Painted pottery deer, goats, naive lions – even an elephant were made in late eighteenth-century Staffordshire by the two Ralph Woods (father and son, 1715-1772 and

1748-1795). As industrialisation crept on apace, potters capitalised on nostalgia for rustic roots. John Walton (c.1780-1835) turned out flocks of sheep and stags beside leafy trees while Obadiah Sherratt (c.1775-1846) depicted the popular sports of bull-baiting and cock- and dog-fighting. Equally collectable are whimsical, anonymous Staffordshire beasts: zebras, spotted and spongeware horses and lustre cats. A china animal with a keen following is the cow, usually fashioned as an earthenware jug (a creamer) after silver originals, with curved tail handle and open mouth spout. The back's lid is often missing. Numerous painted, sponged and printed Staffordshire examples exist, dating from the eighteenth and nineteenth centuries, many of them unmarked.

Animals appealed to porcelain manufacturers too. From the 1820s Rockingham made cats, dogs and rabbits. Woolly-coated sheep and poodles from the 1830s (mostly anonymous) were produced by small Staffordshire porcelain factories such as Samuel Alcock.

**Birds**

With their showy plumage and elegant outlines, birds are irresistibly decorative. Brilliant-hued Chinese porcelain cranes, phoenixes, pheasants, cocks and parrots were exported to Europe from the mid-seventeenth century. Perhaps the most celebrated British collection is Mrs David Gubbay's at Clandon House in Surrey. Some 50 or so seventeenth- and eighteenth-century Chinese birds roost on rococo chinoiserie brackets (themselves carved with birds), often flanking a fireplace. At Drottningholm Palace in Stockholm, the Library of the Chinese Pavilion is decked with Chinese and Japanese birds on tables and in a japanned cabinet.

Birds were popular subjects at Meissen from its earliest years, either copied from Chinese sources or, like the vivid parrots still made, drawn in aviaries. Derby advertised

*above:* a butterfly plate designed by W.S. Coleman for Minton, 1870. *right:* cool cats against stencilled walls at Deerfield, Massachusetts; even in the midst of a patterned environment, these beguiling American pottery creatures make their presence felt as they watch out over the room. Only 'live' creatures have this particular effect.

their winged creations as 'after the finest Dresden models', while Chelsea derived theirs from George Edwards' 'A Natural History of Uncommon Birds'. Birds were employed as painted decoration too, for example at Sèvres. James Rogers at Worcester and the independent decorator James Giles (1718-1780) created vivid fanciful creatures. A century on, in the 1860s and 1870s at Coalport, John Randall (1810-1910) depicted splendid tropical birds. Among the most distinctive modelled birds of the nineteenth century are the Martin Brothers' grotesque tobacco jars. In turn-of-the-century Denmark, Copenhagen was noted for animal and bird models, among them Arnold Krog's simplistic owls and Pietro Krohn's heron service.

Though birds generally look appropriate on a wall, one type, 1930s flying ducks, have been cruelly mocked. Even at the time Carlton made a pastiche of flying toucans to advertise Guinness, with pints balanced on their beaks. From 1935, Worcester produced a limited edition of American and then English birds modelled by Dorothy Doughty (1892-1962). Edward Marshall Boehm made similar models in Trenton, New Jersey between 1955 and 1969. Ann Stokes, a contemporary English potter, creates earthenware owls, eagles and birds of paradise, many with outstretched wings.

### Good reproductions

Infinitely cheaper than eighteenth-century Meissen, and deceptively similar, are the skilful figures, birds and animals made by Emile Samson (1837-1913) of Paris at his father's company, Edmé Samson. The collector is warned against fakes, yet these convincing copies are collected in their own right. Samson made an enormous variety of porcelain, but specialised in eighteenth-century Sèvres, Meissen and Chinese export. His hard-paste versions of soft-paste English figures are more crisply delineated than the originals and decorated with stronger colours. Pieces were stamped with the original's mark and an S – which was sometimes removed in order to deceive. Deceptive forgeries of Chelsea, Derby and Bow figures were made in Torquay in the 1950s and 1960s by Reginald Newland, a restorer.

*left:* a herd of fancifully painted nineteenth-century English cow creamers; designed as novelty jugs for milk or cream, they swiftly became charming, slightly naïve decorative objects; milk maids and calves are more unusual and generally of an earlier date.

127

*below:* a 'covered vase' painted in 1880 by Samson, the great French nineteenth-century fakers of porcelain, in the style of the eighteenth-century English porcelain painter James Giles. *right:* an arrangement of dishes and plates by Brown-Westhead, Moore & Co, to designs by Gustaf Léonce who mainly worked in Limoges but also supplied designs to English pottery firms including Minton and Wedgwood. *following pages, left:* Continental porcelain birds seeemingly in flight up the walls of a house in Seville; *above right:* larger, more earthbound ducks and hens perch precariously above a table laden with eccentric and gaudy botanic ceramics; *below right:* nineteenth-century European pottery money-box birds on top of a wardrobe.

## English pottery figures

The earliest Staffordshire figures were naively modelled salt-glazed men and women on tall upright benches, known as 'pew groups' and made around 1730-45 (now fiendishly expensive). They are often attributed to Aaron Wood, brother and uncle of the two Ralph Woods, the most important makers of English earthenware figures and Toby jugs in the latter eighteenth century. Brightly painted saints, goddesses and pastoral types were made by James Neale of Hanley (1740-1814) and by John Walton from 1806. Also dating from this period are charming pearlware and vivid Prattware figures – the latter named after the Fenton pottery family, with distinctive colouring and moulded relief.

## Victorian Staffordshire figures

Those household gods of the English mantelpiece, Victorian Staffordshire figures (flat-backs), were among the first ornaments aimed at the lower end of the market. They celebrate in pottery form the preoccupations of the masses – royalty, sporting heroes, actresses – just as the tabloid press does today, and were first manufactured around the time of Queen Victoria's marriage in 1840.

Designed for the hearth – hence their flat backs and manufacture in pairs – they vary in height from 20 to 38cm (8 to 15in). Hawkers sold them house to house, at markets and in pleasure grounds. They were ingeniously moulded, often in just two parts, but usually three, at Staffordshire pot-banks, and painted vivid colours – including a dark glossy blue – by children not even in their teens. Many have well-delineated features and combed hair over rough modelling. However the overglaze enamel colours often flake off.

Although popular, even in their heyday Staffordshire flatbacks were looked down on. A cartoon in an 1868 'Punch' depicts a lodger shielding his eyes as he begs his landlady to remove the 'chimney ornam- . . . fictile abominations'. Few museums have good collections. By the early twentieth century anti-Victorian sentiment was riding high; it took several decades before Staffordshire figures began to be appreciated again, as folk art. Some can be seen in the nooks of the painted Bloomsbury stronghold, Charleston Farmhouse in Sussex.

previous pages, main picture: the antique
dealer Keith Skeel's enthusiasm for ceramic
canines extends both to German porcelain pugs
and to Staffordshire pottery poodles (top right),
which he has elegantly set among the leather
books in his bedroom; centre right: Continental
nineteenth-century dogs of rather brighter hue;
bottom right: such was the popularity of
Staffordshire spaniels that, as this jaunty array
in a dog lover's room shows, they were
captured in myriad postures and sizes.
facing page: handsome nineteenth-century
Staffordshire flatbacks, many depicting royal
figures, such as the Empress of France
and Queen Victoria; the fact that their colouring
includes deep blue indicates that they date to
before the 1870s. On the shelf of Victoria
holding a baby are two small German fairings
of people getting into and out of beds – these
are porcelain, while the Staffordshire
figures are pottery. On the bottom row is a
pastille-burner cottage – the smoke is intended
to blow through the chimney.

Staffordshire figures provide a potted history of their day. Queen Victoria and Prince Albert were represented in myriad ways, and their children in carts drawn by goats. (The last royals depicted were Edward VII, Queen Alexandra and Princess May.) The Crimean War alliance between Turkey, England and France led to triple models of the Sultan, Queen Victoria and Emperor Napoleon III; Garibaldi's 1864 visit to England inspired more than a dozen portraits.

From 1860 Staffordshire figures faced competition in the form of even cheaper (and less attractive) hard-paste German 'fairings', which were available as prizes at fairs. These often depict couples in 'ambiguous' situations, for example, in bed. They are still cheap, but not so easily found. Late nineteenth century figures are less bright – often chiefly white and gilt, with only facial markings in full colour. Collectors should beware imitations: even in the later nineteenth century new figures were made from old moulds. Modern reproductions are too perfect, have the wrong palette and fake crazing.

Today Staffordshire figures fetch hundreds (sometimes thousands) of pounds. Having been mass-produced they are plentiful, but there is a great variation of quality and many have suffered minor damage. Most are unmarked, giving collectors a chance to make their own assessment of quality rather than relying on names.

### Victorian Staffordshire dogs

One of the most charming and enduringly popular Staffordshire creations is the Cavalier King Charles spaniel. An absurdly ornamental animal in real life, in china, seated winningly upright, with wig-like floppy ears, large eyes and freckly snout, he is a perfect dish of a dog. This Victorian icon was easy to make, lacking freestanding feet or other complicated potting features. It came in scores of sizes and styles, usually in a pair, with a padlock on the collar and a chain. Spirited large spaniels with copper-lustre patches were produced in Sunderland. Others sport shaggy coats of shredded china or are attached to spill vases (containing tapers for lighting the fire). Most are post-1860. Further Staffordshire canines include slinky ginger greyhounds on royal blue bases, poodles holding baskets and the occasional dalmatian.

*previous pages:* slip-cast porcelain figures and animals by Richard and Susan Parkinson, whose pottery at Brabourne Lees in Kent (1951-63) was among the few British studio potteries to use porcelain in the 1950s.

## English nineteenth-century porcelain figures

Parian ware is an unglazed white porcelain resembling marble which was named after the marble-rich island of Paros – and used almost entirely for busts and figures. It was created around 1846 by Copeland which, along with Worcester and Minton, exhibited Parian figures at the 1851 Great Exhibition; Queen Victoria bought several. In the eighteenth century, figures had been made from unglazed biscuit porcelain (also fired only once), but Parian had a greater glass content and was less easily marked. It was an ideal modelling material, which is why most Parian figures are larger than porcelain ones (30-46cm/12-18in) and of high quality. Cheap Parian imitations of classical statues, portrait busts and winsome poses were mass-produced, and sometimes tinted; John Bell turned out quantities of young girls for Minton. Parian was also made in America, at the Bennington Pottery, and Europe. It is still reasonably priced.

Other figures by nineteenth-century English porcelain factories were largely conventional. One exception was Worcester's modish 'Aesthetic' teapot by James Hadley (1837-1903; best known for sentimental fake-ivory figures): male on one side, female on the other, the spout is one limply raised hand, the other the handle.

## Twentieth-century figures and animals

Twentieth-century artists have had an uneasy relationship with representation: commercial ceramic figures have tended towards the stylised or kitsch, while of artist potters, only Americans have shown sustained fascination for the human figure. However Art Deco's simplified forms translated well into models of animals and figures in smart, undecorated white, cream and black glazes.

In England, Royal Doulton in Staffordshire has produced more than 2,000 bone china figurines since 1913, starting with prim bathing beauties (made by many firms; Rosenthal is the German equivalent). More idiosyncratic figure-makers of the 1920s and 1930s include Gwendolen Parnell, Henry Parr and Charles Vyse. Freelance designers sometimes sold the same design to several

*below left:* a Wedgwood Sea Lion, one of a series of 10 simplified, modernist animals designed by John Skeaping in 1926 to be affordable and made in various bodies and colours; several remained in production into the 1950s. *above:* 1920s porcelain Rosenthal lady with a gazelle; she is a typical elongated, Art Deco figure. *below right:* 'Cat licking its Paw', one of the series of cat mascots – and also a vase – begun by the cat illustrator Louis Wain in 1914.

companies: identical Phoebe Stabler figures were produced by Poole, Ashtead Pottery, and Royal Doulton. This can be confusing.

Modernistic ivory-glaze Art Deco figures formed more of a genre, along with that peculiarly Art Deco fad the wall mask, and were turned out in quantity. The English firm Wade, for example, produced figurines and wall masks by Jessica Van Hallen. Clarice Cliff made dancing couples and musicians. Eric Olsen's figures and animals for Copeland were imitated by Doulton. Doris Lindner fashioned jazzy porcelain figures at Minton, then from 1947 equestrian figures at Worcester (her first was Princess Elizabeth at Trooping of the Colour). In 1930s France, nightlights under translucent porcelain skirts were popular novelties, while German potteries specialised in modish ladies leading borzoi. The Italian company Lenci was known for naked fantasy figures – a lady astride a hippopotamus, or with a baby on a tortoise. In the US the Cowan Pottery studio created Art Deco-esque white figures; the accomplished Waylande Gregory was one designer.

John Skeaping's Art Deco animals for Wedgwood, created as cheap designs after the Depression, are particularly distinguished twentieth-century animals. Skeaping (1901-1980) made 14 studies of which 10 went into production, in several bodies and white, cream and black glazes: a Polar Bear, a Buffalo, a Tiger and Buck, a Duiker antelope standing and one sitting, a Fallow Deer, a Monkey, a Sea Lion, a Bison and a Kangaroo. Other distinctive modern English animals include Louis Wain's robotic 'lucky cats', Arnold Machin's Zodiac Bull for Wedgwood, porcelain animals by Richard and Susan Parkinson and Eve Borthwick's stoneware bull and cow.

Collectors desirous of more contemporary creatures but unable to afford the work of major American potters such as Viola Frey or Akio Takamori can take heart in the UK's wave of affordable figurative ceramics since the 1980s. Among the most singular are Christie Brown's flattened 'classical' figures; large glossy Philip Eglins and Mo Jupp's elongated torsos.

# artist potters

**the strange nineteenth-century world of chemist potters and gorgeous glazes**

After long decades of neglect and contempt, nineteenth-century ceramics can seem exotic and fresh when encountered anew. This is particularly true of work by artist potters. Christopher Dresser's biomorphic-shaped pots look far more modern – and startling – than many by twentieth-century potters. Similarly, the Martin Brothers' grinning, lopsided head-shaped jugs outdo contemporary attempts at anthropomorphic kitsch.

Art potteries making handcrafted wares began to emerge in France, England and America in the 1860s; few survived beyond the First World War. They consisted of a potter-designer (who rarely touched the clay) and his team of craftsmen. Some, like Doulton, were part of an industrial pottery; others were attached to a brick or tile works, while a few depended on the work of an individual such as William De Morgan or Sir Edmund Elton. Simple semi-industrial earthenware shapes predominated, though by the turn of the century a generation of chemist potters ensured that glazes at least were exciting.

The artefacts produced have a curious power in a modern context, separated from the busy, patterned interiors that gave rise to them. Even their often murky palette appears outlandish. This chapter contains a selection of some of the most interesting and collectable European and American makers.

### The lure of history

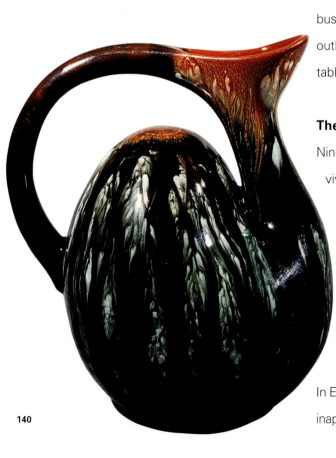

Nineteenth-century ceramics, like all the visual arts, were dominated by historical revivals. In the 1830s and 1840s, the fashion was for Revived Rococo; subsequent borrowings included painted 'Renaissance' maiolica by Doccia and Cantagalli in Italy; versions of sixteenth-century inlaid Henri Deux ware at French and English factories; Spanish mimicking of lustre-painted fifteenth-century Hispano-Moresque wares; relief-moulded 'Gothic' English stoneware jugs; even 'classical' pots – at the 1851 Great Exhibition in London, for example, Thomas Battram displayed Greek-style vases tumbling from an 'Etruscan' tomb.

In England, the most industrialised European country, there was growing disquiet at the inappropriate use of historical motifs and the effect on design of mass-production and

*left:* a camel-backed vase designed by Christopher Dresser for Linthorpe Pottery in the early 1880s. Dresser's curious asymmetrical ceramics drew on many influences, but particularly Japan and South America. *right:* an 1893 stoneware Martin Brothers' 'Wallybird' tobacco jar, named after Robert Wallace Martin, the eldest brother, and the modeller of the family.

mechanisation. The ornamental excesses of the Great Exhibition spurred writers on art such as John Ruskin, William Morris and Henry Cole to seek out a new aesthetic in which form and ornament would be united. The Arts and Crafts movement was the result, promoting the creation of individual, hand-made objects true to their material and function.

## William De Morgan

William De Morgan (1839-1917), England's first independent artist potter, was encouraged to take up the decorative arts by William Morris. His swirling large-scale flowers, fabulous beasts and foliate patterns make his work instantly recognisable; they were inspired by medieval and Middle Eastern motifs and have some similarities with Morris's own designs. Morris's daughter May wrote that 'the special bent of De Morgan's invention was in winding beast forms and great sweeping lines round difficult shapes; the more difficult the space to be filled and the more fantastic the beast pattern, the more enjoyment is evident'. The strong-hued palette and stylised patterns of his pottery translates well into the modern interior.

In the 1860s De Morgan designed stained glass and tiles for Morris's company, Morris, Marshall, Faulkner & Co. In 1872 he moved to Chelsea, and over the next decade made some 300 tile designs. He experimented with metallic pigments to revive antique ruby and gold lustre; then devised singing blue glazes and blue and green Persian and Iznik-style designs. He made copies of Islamic

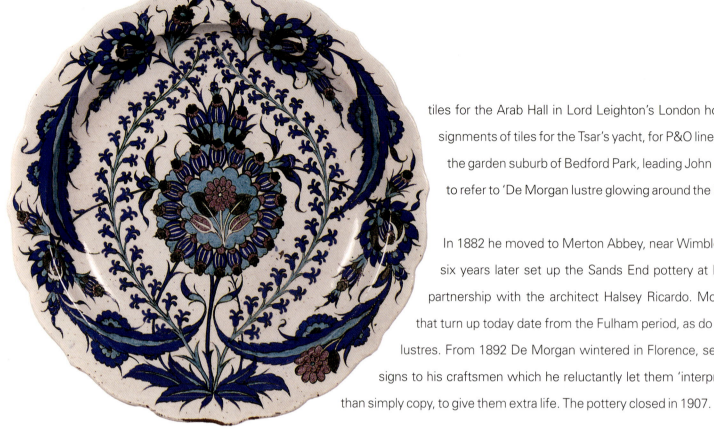

tiles for the Arab Hall in Lord Leighton's London home, consignments of tiles for the Tsar's yacht, for P&O liners, and for the garden suburb of Bedford Park, leading John Betjeman to refer to 'De Morgan lustre glowing around the hearth'.

In 1882 he moved to Merton Abbey, near Wimbledon, and six years later set up the Sands End pottery at Fulham in partnership with the architect Halsey Ricardo. Most pieces that turn up today date from the Fulham period, as do the finest lustres. From 1892 De Morgan wintered in Florence, sending designs to his craftsmen which he reluctantly let them 'interpret' rather than simply copy, to give them extra life. The pottery closed in 1907.

*previous pages:* an arrangement of mid-nineteenth century neo-classical vases by Staffordshire potteries such as Samuel Alcock and Hill Pottery. In the centre of the lower shelf is a version of the Wedgwood Portland vase which inspired much of the vases' imagery; their bases contain the subject's original title. *this page, above:* 'Damascus-style' leaves and patterns painted on an earthenware dish in 1865 by the French glaze master Théodore Deck; *right:* Islamic themes were taken up in England by William De Morgan, as in the Iznik colours and motifs of this long-necked vase of c. 1890, when his pottery was based in Fulham.

## Christopher Dresser and the influence of Japan

Perhaps the greatest long-term impact on ceramics came from Japan, isolated from the West for 150 years until the 1850s. The display of Japanese arts at the 1862 International Exhibition in London provided western designers with a new vocabulary of shapes and decoration – in the case of ceramics, moon vases, rich yellows, bright twig-ware, asymmetry and fewer border-patterns. Minton and Royal Worcester soon created wares inspired by Japanese artefacts.

One of Minton's designers, and possibly the greatest exponent of the arts of Japan, was Christopher Dresser (1834-1904). For him, the excitement of the Japanese exhibition turned into a life-long passion, both as a writer on the decorative arts and as a designer in many media. A trained botanical artist, Dresser incorporated stylised Japanese butterflies, grasshoppers and flying cranes into his work. Though espousing the belief that objects should be functional and simple, some of his designs for Minton, such as turquoise Cloisonné, based on enamelled metal Japanese vases, seem impossibly sumptuous. Among the other companies he designed ceramics for were Wedgwood, Old Hall Earthenware Co and Watcombe Terra Cotta Co.

In 1878, while visiting the Linthorpe Brick Works in Middlesbrough, Yorkshire, Dresser suggested using the clay there to make pottery. The following year Linthorpe Pottery was born, with Dresser as art director (for three years) and Henry Tooth manager. It sought to mass-produce art pottery at reasonable prices and was a great success. Many of Dresser's 500 or so designs for Linthorpe have a simple sculptural quality – elongated double gourds, for instance. He incorporated features from pottery he had seen in Japan, creating dimpled, folded and asymmetrical forms which he gave figured glazes or electric yellow, red, purple and green ones similar to Awaji pottery.

Linthorpe also produced incised, pierced and relief pots, and more conventional pieces painted with flowers and birds. Dresser designed examples of both. He insisted that all pots be thrown – to give them vitality – and then shaped. Apart from Japan, he drew on Celtic, pre-Columbian, Mexican, Egyptian and Roman influences; his head-shaped vase with a bar across its two spouts is Peruvian in inspiration; its incised features and experimental running mottled glaze are very much his own.

Dresser's designs were also produced at the Bretby Art Pottery, which Henry Tooth founded with William Ault in 1883, and later at the Ault Pottery, which Ault founded in 1887 (both were in Derbyshire). After Linthorpe closed in 1889, Ault bought up the Linthorpe moulds at auction and continued to make 'Dresser' pots – to which he often added his own shimmering glazes – even after Dresser died in 1904. Dresser's space-agey shapes and powerful glazes have dated well. The British artists Gilbert and George are among those who collect them.

### Pioneer French potters

The country with the most advanced glaze technology in the mid-nineteenth century was France. In 1861, the glaze virtuoso Théodore Deck (1823-1891), inspired by near-Eastern glazes, concocted a turquoise that became known as *bleu de Deck*. Deck also encouraged artists like Félix Bracquemond and Eléonore Escallier to decorate pottery with naturalistic scenes in the Japanese style. Bracquemond went on to use devices from Japanese prints on the

*left:* a collection of William De Morgan lustreware dishes, all designed by him but executed by assistants including Fred and Charles Passenger and Joe Juster. Beneath them, Howsons flambé ware of 1912 flanks a pair of lustre Burmantofts vases; in the centre is a *flambé* Foh dog by Bernard Moore. *below left:* a group of French *ceramiques impressionistes* from the 1870s and 1880s, first introduced by Ernest Chaplet while working for Laurin at Bourg-la-Reine. *right:* a magnificent charger by Eléonore Escallier for Théodore Deck surrounded by paintings and a ceramic relief panel by Robert Anning Bell. The charger is similar to one shown at the Paris International exhibition of 1867 and now in the Victoria & Albert Museum. The other ceramics are all French, by studio potters including Ernst Chaplet, Auguste Delaherche, and André Metthey. The brass and copper fender is by W.A.S. Benson and the silver figure is of Barnavar the Beautiful by Alexander Fisher.

*Top, above and right:* a magnificent collection of Linthorpe wares by Christopher Dresser close-up and *in situ*. The different arrangement and extra pots in the dresser full of Dressers at *right* are a reminder of how collectors love to rearrange and add to their collections.

*right:* a busy and thoroughly modern mix of old and new in the drawing room of the interior designer Anthony Collett. Streaky-glazed Bretby vases are grouped on the dresser, in front of contemporary oriental panels, and on the fire-place. In the foreground stands a terracotta temple by Alison Neville and a tall 'grass' vase by Bretby – for displaying pampas grass. *below:* a lustrous vase decorated by Richard Joyce for Pilkington's Royal Lancastrian; he worked there from 1905 until his death in 1931 and painted more Lancastrian ware than any other artist.

fresh-looking faience table service he designed for Creil, positioning simply coloured, outlined cocks, insects and flowers off-centre against a plain ground. From the 1880s Deck made deep-red flambé glazes and used gold as a background colour on tableware. In 1887 he was the first potter to be appointed art director at Sèvres.

The most influential late nineteenth-century French glaze technician was Ernest Chaplet (1835-1909), who developed the 'barbotine' method of painting in coloured slips while at Haviland-Auteuil. From the late 1880s he devoted himself to simple, Chinese-shaped vases with rich crimson glazes. He also fired the pottery of his friend Paul Gauguin. Other turn-of-the-century potters influenced by his work include Auguste Delaherche, Albert Dammouse and Adrien Dalpayat.

### British chemist potters

In Britain too, a generation of chemist potters took up the glaze challenge, creating a brilliant turquoise blue in the 1880s, followed by the more technically difficult red *flambé* and *sang de boeuf.* Between them, the Burton brothers at Pilkington, Bernard Moore, and William Howson Taylor at the Ruskin Pottery devised some of the most sumptuous glazes ever.

**Pilkington**: The technical wizard at Pilkington Tile and Pottery Co, near Manchester (founded 1891), was William Burton, assisted by his brother Joseph, who made first tiles and then decorated art pottery there. From 1903, simple shapes were thrown and glazed with glittering Sunstone, Eggshell, uranium orange or vermilion. Iridescent lustre was painted on already glazed wares, giving them a glassy look.

In 1906 the dynamic Gordon Forsyth became chief artist (until the First World War) alongside W.S. Mycock, Gwladys Rodgers, Richard Joyce, Walter Crane and C.F.A. Voysey. From 1908, lively painting in lustre predominated – of heraldic designs, Grecian warriors, animals and flowers. In 1913 Pilkington received a royal warrant and became Pilkington's Royal Lancastrian. Lustre painting ceased in 1928, but the art pottery carried on until 1938, and tile-making until it merged with Poole Pottery in 1964.

**Ruskin Pottery**: Equally refulgent were the high-fired wares and reduction glazes of Ruskin Pottery at Smethwick, near Birmingham (which ran from 1898 to 1935). Reduction glazes are produced when the oxygen in the kiln is reduced, thereby conjuring up all kinds of colours and textures. For the first decade the firm was known as the Birmingham Tile and Pottery Works; John Ruskin's executor and niece, Mrs Arthur Severn, was eventually persuaded by the pottery's wares to lend it the name of Ruskin. Its founder and guiding light, William Howson Taylor (1876-1935), was a keen disciple of John Ruskin.

His other passion was Sung and Ming dynasty pottery whose glazes he tried to emulate. Most Ruskin wares are of plain form decorated only with glazes, which gives them a contemporary feel. They can be divided into monochrome-glazed soufflé wares; lustrewares in every hue; and experimental high-fired wares, the outcome of which it was hard to predict – how mottled or freckled, or the colour of viridian spots created by copper salts. The recipes, which Taylor destroyed before he died, were a close secret.

**Bernard Moore**: Another producer of 'glowing' glazes was the ceramic chemist Bernard Moore (1850-1935), who in 1870, with his brother Samuel (died 1890), took on their father's factory at Longton in Staffordshire. At the turn of the century he began to research oriental and Middle Eastern glaze techniques, and went on to produce a fine *flambé* – which he flecked with 'golden lights' – turquoise glazes and lustres. From 1905 to 1915 Moore ran his own decorating studio in Stoke-on-Trent. His crystalline glazes on plain shapes were often decorated with underglaze flowers, flying birds, fish and Viking vessels. The artists, who included Dora Billington and John Adams (later director of the Poole Pottery), generally signed their work.

**Moorcroft**: William Moorcroft (1872-1945) is best known for his Florian Ware, which he launched a year after taking charge of the art pottery at James Macintyre & Co of Burslem, Stoke-on-Trent, in 1898. In it, stylised flowers and leaves are outlined in white slip then painted, usually blue or green. Florian Ware and

*below left:* a Bernard Moore lidded jar with crystalline glaze and dragon painted by Hilda Beardmore, one of the artists Moore employed at his decorating studio between 1905 and 1914. *right:* a Moorcroft vase in Moonlit Blue, launched in 1922; William Moorcroft was an excellent glaze chemist. His designs consisted chiefly of slip-trailed outlines into which colour was added; rich blue proved particularly popular.

versions such as Pomegranate and Pansy sold worldwide for decades; trailed-outline land-scapes were also popular.

In 1913, with the backing of the Liberty family, Moorcroft set up on his own at Cobridge, Stoke-on-Trent. He introduced new lines such as speckled Powder Blue tableware – produced until the 1960s – and made simpler, bolder floral designs. He devoted his last 20 years to developing *flambé* glazes, which won many awards. His son Walter took over in 1945 and retired only in 1986. Though output was commercial and high, Moorcroft is expensive, and has a keen following.

### Industrial art potters

**Doulton**: The first commercial factory in England to bring in outside artists was Doulton in Lambeth, which owed its success to the manufacture of stoneware drainage pipes. In the 1860s, the head of Lambeth School of Art encouraged Henry Doulton (1820-1897) to set up an art-pottery department, to which he would supply students. The first student, George Tinworth (1843-1913), was recruited in 1866, and over the next 47 years produced a steady stream of salt-glazed stoneware incised with foliate designs and dotted relief (like most Doulton wares in a restrained palette of blues and browns), along with terracotta plaques, numerous boy musicians, and frog and mice groups in-dulging in various human activites.

In 1871, he was joined by Hannah Barlow, and later by her brother Arthur and sister Florence. (Many women artists were employed.) Hannah specialised in sgraffito animal designs and her sister in birds. Other Doulton artists to look out for include the inventive Frank Butler (whose work was collected by Queen Victoria and William Gladstone), Eliza Simmance who made Art Nouveau-style flower and fruit decorations, and from 1880

*right:* a display of the fabulously detailed salt-glazed stoneware produced by Doulton from the 1870s to the early 1900s. The circular plaque, 'Foxes have holes and the birds of the air have nests', is by George Tinworth, and was exhibited at the 1876 Philadelphia Centennial Exhibition. The terracotta relief on the left, 'So near but yet so far', by Hannah Barlow, was shown at the Royal Academy. The centre piece on the cabinet is by Mark V. Marshall, a superb modeller, as are the majority of the flanking pieces and those in the picture on the *left*, dating to 1890-1905. *below left:* more startling pots – the two grotesque jugs on the left are by Blanche Vuilliamy, c.1900; on the right is a whimsical jug by Leroy Burket, an American potter who lived in France.

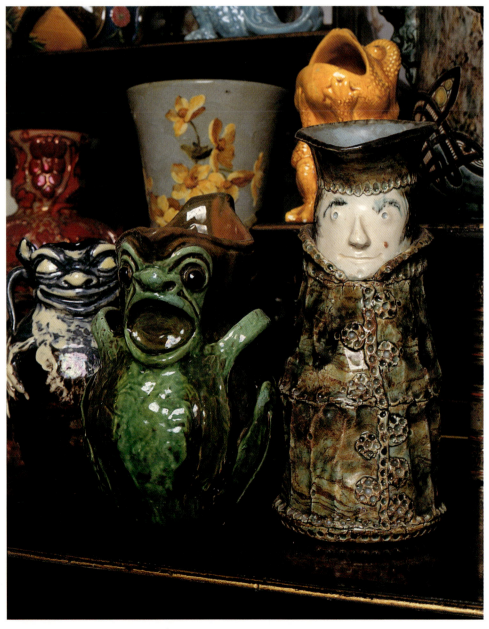

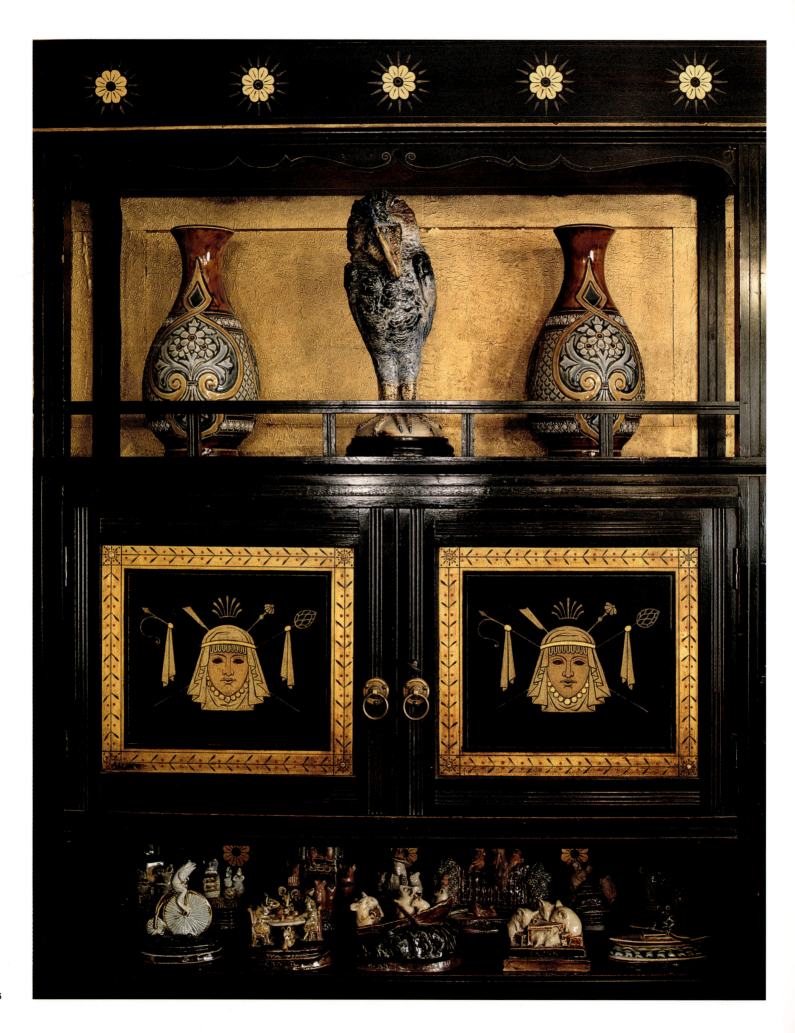

*left:* the salt-glazed ceramics displayed on an ebonised Godwin-style cabinet are the work of the Martin Brothers and George Tinworth. The collection of humorous mouse and frog groups by George Tinworth were done as light relief from his devout religious works; their titles include 'Cockneys at Brighton', 'Teatime Scandal' and 'Drunk'. The bird perched on the upper shelf is by Wallace Martin, flanked by a pair of Doulton vases. *below right:* an earthenware Della Robbia vase slip-decorated by Liza Wilkins, 1903.

Mark V. Marshall, a superb modeller who created grotesques, scrolling dragons and other animals. Faience was made by a separate group from 1873.

**Minton**: In 1871 Minton opened an art pottery studio in Kensington, where artists decorated biscuit wares from the Stoke-on-Trent factory. Although it lasted only four years, painted plaques by such artists as W.S. Coleman and Henry Stacey Marks form a distinctive genre.

### Individual artist potters

The Martin Brothers: Robert Wallace (1843-1923), Charles (1846-1910), Walter (1859-1912) and Edwin (1860-1915) Martin worked together for over 30 years from 1873, creating distinctive salt-glazed stoneware of great imagination. Each brother had his specialty: Wallace was the director and modeller; Walter the chief thrower, in charge of firing and glazing; Edwin concentrated on decoration; Charles handled the business side. They all did some designing and decoration.

In 1877 the pottery moved to Southall in west London, and the following year the brothers opened a shop (which Charles managed) in Holborn. At first they made simple conventional wares, but from 1880 they began to incise and carve ornate designs on more robust shapes. Their colours, always muted, moved from blues and greys to greens, cobalt blues and browns.

Edwin's incised decoration (some 85 patterns) ranged from Doulton-like ducks to intricate Renaissance scrolling and Art Nouveau-esque flowers, particularly foxgloves. Wallace – an eccentric religious figure who had assisted Pugin at the Houses of Parliament – is known for his grotesques, especially the big-beaked bird tobacco jars with

*left:* an array of eccentric and bizarre pieces in a 'nature' room, including stuffed animals, birds, fish, and arrangements of birds' eggs, butterflies, shell boxes and frames. The central plate with a white-background depicts a Death's Head moth, a caterpillar and other curious items; it is labelled 'The Darwin theory explained, what is Man?' and signed Jos. Crawhall. This satirical jibe also inspired the collection of 'barking and grunting' pieces which crowd the cabinet. The teapots are by Minton and the beehive by George Jones.

detachable heads ('Wallybirds'), which appeared from the early 1880s, and the double-sided grinning 'face jugs', later mass-produced by other firms. From 1895 Edwin developed a series of ribbed vegetable ware in a more restrained Japanese style.

After Charles died in 1910 production declined, and ceased four years later. (The Martinware made until the 1930s by Wallace's son Clement is of inferior quality.) The output consisted mainly of vases and pots, from miniature to large, all signed, and each one different. Although not popular in their lifetime, they are now valued and expensive.

**The potting baronet**: After a first career as an inventor, Sir Edmund Elton (1846-1920) set up the Sunflower Pottery in 1879, making purely decorative pottery. It was called Elton Ware from 1882. Using clay from his estate at Clevedon Court in Somerset, Elton fashioned heavy pots with layers of rich-coloured slip on which he painted – or applied in relief – chrysanthemums or sunflowers.

From 1902 he creating crazed all-over metallic 'craqueleware' glazes in which the ground colours sometimes show through. Shapes were simple or highly complex – influenced by South American and African pots, with contorted spouts and squashed rims. After Elton died his son carried on the pottery for ten years. The craqueleware in particular is distinctive and collectable.

### Other British art potteries

The Della Robbia pottery at Birkenhead – named after fifteenth-century Della Robbia maiolica in Florence – produced art pottery from 1894 to 1906. Some wares imitated maiolica using coloured enamels, but more often they combined sgraffito and painting, with incised outlines round Art Nouveau-esque plant forms. A team of artists ensured high-quality decoration.

Burmantofts (c.1880-1904), attached to a brickworks outside Leeds, made architectural faience before venturing into slip-decorated tiles and elaborately moulded vases and jardinières. Early pieces were often bulbous with long necks and streaky glazes; snakes and lizards twisted round vases.

From the 1850s to 1970 Maw & Co in Shropshire specialised in painted and embossed tiles and mosaics. Their William De Morgan-style lustrewares date from the late 1870s and boast galleons galore. In the early 1880s, some ruby lustre vases and ewers were decorated with figures and sailing ships by Walter Crane. Among more affordable pieces are coloured slipware by Devon potters such as Aller Vale Pottery and C.H. Brannam's bold sgraffito 'Barum Ware'.

## Art Nouveau

From the 1880s tendrils, sinuous flowers and leafs began to curl round metalwork, glass and ceramics. The style was termed Art Nouveau in England and America, *stile Liberty* in Italy and Jugendstil in Germany and Scandinavia. At Sèvres, Théodore Deck brought in artists and architects such as Hector Guimard to design Art Nouveau wares. Other European exponents included Rörstrand in Sweden, Cantagalli in Italy, and above all Rozenburg in The Hague, where J. Jurian Kok gave floral decoration to tapering porcelain forms. William Moorcroft and the Martin Brothers were English exponents of the style.

*left:* a stoneware vase with exaggerated curves (1902) by the Belgian designer Henri van de Velde, an influential figure in the Art Nouveau and Modern movements. *right:* a high-fired stoneware vase (1914) by Ruskin Pottery, originally owned by the pottery's founder, W. Howson Taylor. The deliciously rich, mottled surface, inspired by Chinese glazes, was experimental – no two came out the same.

*right:* a mammoth turn-of-the-century dresser-cum-cabinet is the perfect setting for large scale art pottery. Chunky vessels by Old Hall Earthenware Co sit solidly between the top row of zingingly turquoise Minton ewers and vases and, behind glass doors, gold craqueleware by Sir Edmund Elton, with a crazed all-over metallic glaze. *below:* a Rookwood earthenware jar decorated in coloured slips by Harriet Wilcox and exhibited at the Paris Exhibition of 1900, where Rookwood won a grand prix.

## American artist potters

**Rookwood**: The first major art pottery in America was Rookwood, in Cincinnati, Ohio, set up by Maria Longworth Nichols in 1880. She and Mary Louise McLaughlin had become interested in china painting in the 1870s, and exhibited wares at the 1876 Philadelphia Centennial Exhibition. The most admired pieces there were Japanese ceramics, and high-gloss Haviland-Auteuil barbotine wares. Briefly the rage in Europe, in America these became the basis of the artist-pottery movement.

McLaughlin experimented to achieve the barbotine effect, which, adopted by Rookwood, became known as Cincinnati Limoges or faience. During the 1880s, Rookwood acquired an international reputation, simplified its forms and colours, and devised a method of spraying glaze ('Rookwood standard'). Japanese-style flora and fauna in earthy colours was its chief decoration – Art Nouveau-style after 1900. A distinctive series of vases (1897-1903) bear photographic portraits of American Indians. Barbotine wares were also produced at the Chelsea Keramic Art Works, outside Boston.

**Other major American art potteries**: The Newcomb College Pottery in New Orleans was set up in emulation of Rookwood in 1896 to teach young women, and later began to market its wares. Its incised Art Nouveau motifs, many by Mary G. Sheerer, were restricted to flora and fauna of the southern States, and its palette to blue, green, yellow and black. Other companies developed matt glazes. At the Grueby Faience Company in Boston, Massachusetts (founded 1894), William Grueby created yellow, brown and particularly green glazes, which he applied to leaf-covered surfaces. The Teco pottery of Terra Cotta, Illinois used matt glazes on simple organic forms, as did Tiffany from 1904 on moulded Art Nouveau-flavour Favrile pottery.

Other pioneering American potters include Mary Chase Perry (1867-1961), who created iridescent lustres at the Pewabic Pottery she established in Detroit in 1903, Adelaide Alsop Robineau (1865-1929), who carved extraordinarily intricate porcelain vases, and the eccentric George Ohr (1857-1918) of Biloxi, Mississippi, inventor of unctuous, mottled glazes who manipulated clay into bizarre shapes, some of them 1.8m (6ft) high.

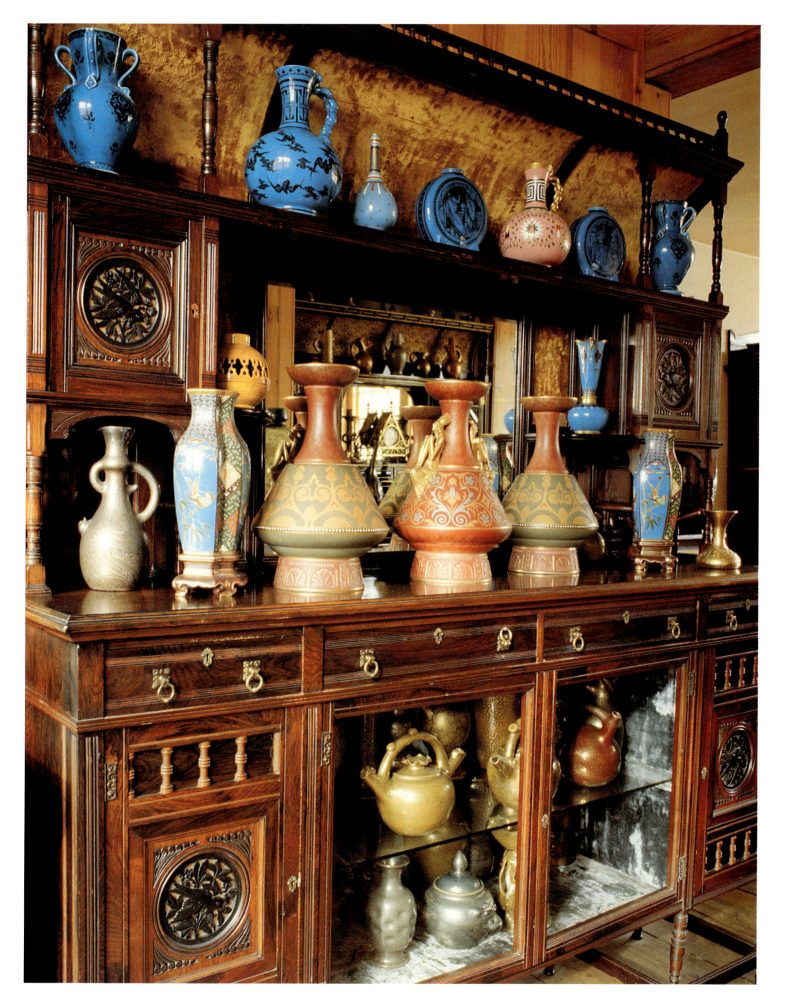

# twentieth-century pottery

**a thoroughly modern mélange of studio potters and factory finery**

Desirable twentieth-century ceramics exist in dizzy-making profusion. Thanks to the march of the machine age and the apparently contradictory desire for the one-off and hand-crafted, two separate traditions have prospered: that of the individual potter and the manufacturing industry. This chapter concentrates on the more romantic studio potter, while touching on factory finery from the 1920s to the 1960s. The term studio pottery first appeared in the mid-1920s to differentiate the work of the art potter, who designs his work but has it made by someone else, and the 'studio' potter, who both designs and makes it.

Much western studio pottery since the First World War is characterised by a powerful simplicity of form. To take one example: a Lucie Rie vase with a long, slim neck flaring out into a wide rounded lip has a grace and force that is self-contained and magnetic. Such an object will work in almost any context: as a hand-made shape in a minimalist setting; providing a moment of stillness to a busier, more old-fashioned one.

Items by icon potters such as Bernard Leach and Hans Coper can be found at auction and in craft shops; though increasingly expensive they still cost less than work by artists of a similar calibre in other fields. It is usually possible to buy direct from a potter (at a lower price than in a shop) and to commission pieces – a thrilling process that instantly establishes a connection between the maker, the pot and the buyer.

### England: from the early twentieth century

Little adventurous pottery was attempted in England before the First World War. The art potter's preoccupation with rich glazes continued, while the other prevalent influence was medieval oriental stoneware – recently unearthed pieces from Tang and Sung tombs were shown in London to great acclaim; potters such as William Staite Murray and Reginald Wells imitated their simple shapes and natural-coloured glazes. During the 1920s and 1930s the oriental stoneware aesthetic was propounded and followed by two schools, the first embodied by Murray who regarded pottery as an art somewhere between painting and sculpture, and the second by Bernard Leach who believed that a pot's beauty – and integrity – depended on its usefulness.

## William Staite Murray

William Staite Murray (1881-1962) was by far the most significant of the proto-studio potters. In spite of the plainness of his pots (nearly always vases and bowls), he had no interest in useful wares. He exhibited only in West End galleries, alongside painters like Christopher Wood and Ben Nicholson, charging fine-art prices – an unheard-of 100 guineas for a *sang-de-boeuf* vase in 1927, for example. Murray was an extremely skilled thrower. The scale of his beautifully controlled, elongated vases has rarely been matched since; their decoration is minimal – mostly stone-coloured glazes with occasional oriental brushwork. From 1925 to 1940 he was Professor of Ceramics at the Royal College of Art. When the Second World War broke out he and his wife were in Southern Rhodesia where they remained for the rest of his life. Murray never potted again.

## Bernard Leach

The strong oriental flavour of studio pottery in England – and later America – since the 1920s is due in large part to Bernard Leach (1887-1979), the century's most famous potter. His love affair with the Far East began during his childhood in Japan, Hong Kong and Singapore, where his father was a colonial barrister. After school in England and art school in London, he returned to Japan in 1910, to teach etching. He was introduced to pottery at a 'raku' party where guests decorated bowls which were then glazed and fired.

Thrilled by the possibilities of clay, he searched out a master potter and trained with him for two years. He visited China and Korea where he was moved by simple stoneware which he sought to emulate. On returning to Britain in 1920 he set up a pottery near St Ives in Cornwall with a young Japanese potter called Shoji Hamada (1894-1978). They made Japanese-style stoneware, but also became fascinated by traditional English slipware.

Like Murray, Leach exhibited in Bond Street galleries, though when it became apparent that high prices were putting off all but rich clients, he

*left:* stoneware 'Monad with square' by Gordon Baldwin, 1987. *above:* 'The Bather', 1930, by William Staite Murray, an expert thrower who regarded pottery as an art somewhere between painting and sculpture, unlike Bernard Leach, who believed that making pots was a serious moral activity; both were inspired by Far Eastern ceramics and worked principally in thrown stonewares with glaze effects. *right:* stoneware 'fish' vase by Leach.

devised more functional ware. His son David (born 1911), who had joined him in 1930, set up a production pottery at St Ives. The standard ware – in tenmoku, celadon and painted oatmeal – was continued after Bernard's death into the 1980s by his third wife, Janet.

A huge number of potters came into contact with Leach during almost 60 years at St Ives; some went on to teach a new generation of potters. Among the best known were Hamada and Michael Cardew. Other early students were Katharine Pleydell-Bouverie and Norah Braden. It was only after the Second World War that Leach achieved great popular success. The turning point was his seminal 'A Potter's Book' (1940), which laid out his belief in the moral and spiritual dimensions of pottery. It was the first do-it-yourself book for potters and has been in print ever since.

While Leach's shapes – sometimes, under his instruction, thrown by others – are simple and sturdy, their painted or incised decoration is sensitive and controlled. His work fits into rather than dominates a room; having been out of fashion for some decades, it is still reasonably affordable. Leach's belief in 'good honest pots' and the beauty of the everyday informed several generations of domestic potters (and much speckly brown tableware). Small potteries started up all over Britain, and beyond. By the 1970s there was a widespread reaction against the oriental influence. This was when the brash, uninhibited work of American potters began to have such an impact.

### Factory finery

In the 1920s and 1930s, while studio potters looked to the Orient, commercial potters in Europe revelled in abstract patterns, geometric shapes and strident colours. Such exuberance was damped down by the Second World War, but reasserted itself in the early 1950s, when spiky patterns, strong hues and biomorphic shapes came to the fore. England alone played for the mass-market, producing cheap, colourful tableware decorated with watered-down modernist elements. Still affordable and obtainable, this holds its own in contemporary interiors. Work by named designers can be found at auction, while pieces by lesser-known factories (some 400 in 1930s Stoke-on-Trent alone) turn up in charity shops.

Streamlined Art Deco (its name taken from the 1925 Paris Exposition Internationale des Arts Décoratifs et Industriels Modernes – though it was known as 'Art Deco' only from the 1960s) flourished between the end of the First and the beginning of the Second World War. It is a loosely applied term referring to aerodynamic, machine-made shapes and stylized geometric decoration – a mish-mash of Fauvism, Cubism and Futurism tempered with theatrical input from the Ballets Russes and Ancient Egypt (Tutankhamun's tomb was discovered in 1922).

### English Art Deco ceramics

In an England desperate for trade after the 1926 General Strike, bright tea wares in gimmicky shapes proliferated, although regarded as kitsch even at the time. Bevis Hillier called it 'the folk art of the machine age'. There was also a revival of hand-painted wares. A.E. Gray, in Hanley early on produced lustre-painted pieces; among the paintresses it employed from local art schools was Susie Cooper (1902-1995), who joined in 1922.

**Susie Cooper**: In 1929 Cooper founded her own decorating business, and three years later produced her first acclaimed curvy, modernist shapes, Kestrel. As the decade progressed her decoration became more restrained and she began to use subtle pinks, yellows, browns and greys. Among her techniques were drawing with colour sticks, as in Crayon Loop, and spray-gun aerography. By the mid-1930s she had developed lithographic transfers that looked like hand-painting, enabling her to mass-produce patterns from leaping deer to pastel florals. The technique was soon copied. Keeping pace with changing tastes, she thrived in the 1940s and 1950s. In 1966 the company was subsumed by Wedgwood, for whom she was chief designer for six years.

**Clarice Cliff**: The boldest, most recognisable ceramics of the era are the crude, outlined designs by Clarice Cliff (1899-1972). Apprenticed at the age of 13, Cliff joined the firm of A.J. Wilkinson in Burslem four years later. In 1920 Wilkinson took over the nearby Newport Pottery, and Cliff began to paint experimental patterns of garish

*top left:* a sequence of vases by the Dutch designer Jan des Bouvrie on chunky wood blocks in Saint Tropez. *left:* 1950s pots in New York, their rounded forms accentuated by spindly lights. *above:* Fornasetti and other red crocks stand out bright and strong against a Victorian corner cupboard in Sue Timney's home. *top right:* Adam and Eve plates (1954) by Fornasetti, in a French farmhouse. *right:* a head by Oriel Harwood in a London home. *far right:* a ceramic display along the back of a sofa – from left, by John Ward, Betty Blandino, Aki Moriuchi, Ward, Bernard Rooke and Annie Fourmanoir; above is a sculpture by Emilio Greco, and ceramics by Poh Chap Yeap, John Ward and Picasso.

jazz-age colours and diluted cubist shapes on undecorated stock. The 'Bizarre' patterns, as Cliff christened them, did well when tested – and even better after a rare publicity campaign in 1928.

Such extreme designs cried out for shapes to match them. The first, Conical (1929), was tapering with solid triangular handles and feet. Between 1929 and 1934 several shapes and an enormous variety of decorations and colour schemes were launched. These ranged from bold geometrics (triangular Sunray and Umbrellas & Rain) and all-over abstracts to stylised florals, the most successful of which was the first, Crocus, and simple landscapes. By the late 1930s the designs were simpler and the florals more traditional. All are now rare and expensive.

Another forward-looking company was Shelley, whose modern designs came (untypically) in bone china rather than earthenware. Their shapes veer from the sleek steep cones and triangular handles of Vogue and Mode (both 1930) to traditional Queen Anne (1926) painted with chocolate-box Cottage Garden. Simple, curvy Regent (1932) with hollow ring handles proved enduringly popular, as did Mabel Lucie Atwell's nurseryware (toadstool-house teapots). Whimsical 1930s wares by other factories include Burleigh's bird-handled jugs, John Beswick's Cottage tableware (made from 1934 to 1971), and Carlton Ware's decorative and novelty tea wares.

**British artists and ceramics**

In a different vein, the Bloomsbury artists Duncan Grant and Vanessa Bell painted original, fresh designs on simple shapes for Roger Fry's Omega Workshop, which ran for a few years from 1913. (Vanessa's son Quentin took up pottery in the 1930s and for over 60 years turned out colourful high-spirited wares.) In 1934, Clarice Cliff collaborated with 26 artists to produce tableware for E. Brain for an exhibition at Harrods; artists included Barbara Hepworth, Graham Sutherland, Paul Nash, Duncan Grant and Ben Nicholson. Laura Knight's Circus, the most traditional design, was also the most popular. Another artist who designed affordable 'good' ceramics was Frank Brangwyn (1867-1956). His

moulded, incised services for Doulton – each piece different – were launched in 1930 and produced till the Second World War. The most successful, Harvest, consisted of softly outlined fruit and flowers. It was not a commercial success.

**Wedgwood**

Wedgwood used freelance artists for their printed wares. In the early 1930s Rex Whistler (1905-1944) produced Clovelly, while from 1935 Eric Ravilious (1903-1942) made finely drawn tableware designs, many put into production several years after his death while working as a war artist. These were printed, then hand-tinted: looping Persephone (1938) was printed in grey and tinted yellow, green or blue. Ravilious's designs blend English domesticity – greenhouses, wheelbarrows, afternoon tea – and precise machine-made delineation on plain ceramic shapes. His first piece was the firework, lion and unicorn Coronation Mug, designed for Edward VIII but quickly adapted for George VI and later Elizabeth II.

*above:* Laura Knight's Circus plate. It was designed for an exhibition of ceramics by artists in 1934, organised by Clarice Cliff. *top:* a plate with a lustre design similar to those produced by A.E. Gray. *right:* Burleigh bird jug, designed by Charles Wilkes in the 1930s and made until the 1950s. *left:* a Fantasque conical milk jug by Clarice Cliff, painted with the Melon pattern in the 1930s. It is typical of the innovative angular forms she developed to suit her jazzy Bizzare decorations.

Wedgwood also championed hand-painting, in 1926 opening a hand-painting studio at the Etruria factory at Stoke-on-Trent. One of the best paintresses was Millicent Taplin, whose neat, pretty designs often employ lustre. Victor Skellern, the young director from 1934, produced lively, simple patterns such as Snow Crystals (1936) and Astral (1938). At the factory proper, intricate Fairyland Lustre by Daisy Makeig-Jones (1881-1945) enjoyed great popularity from 1915 to the late 1920s.

Wedgwood's most admired inter-war ceramics were ribbed vases by Keith Murray (1892-1981), a New Zealand architect who also designed silver and glass. From 1933 to 1946 he worked at Wedgwood for three months a year (in 1938 he designed their new factory at Barlaston, outside Stoke-on-Trent). His mostly ornamental earthenware was decorated in matt and satin glazes – Moonstone, Grey, Straw, Green – devised by Norman Wilson, Wedgwood's creative works manager.

*right:* a cache of Poole pottery stacked smartly and tightly in the bathroom of John Clark of Art Deco Etc. The vases with red stars on the bottom shelf are part of the Contemporary range (1953-54), while the more biomorphic shapes are Free Form (introduced in 1956) with patterns by Ruth Pavely; the shapes were all designed in the 1950s by Alfred Read and Guy Sydenham. *left:* the Poole plaques over the fireplace were designed and painted by Ann Read in 1955 and 1956. The vases on the mantelpiece are also Poole, with Ruth Pavely designs on Alfred Read and Guy Sydenham shapes. *below left:* Poole 'Atlantis' ware, designed by Guy Sydenham and made between 1972 and 1977.

## Lucie Rie and Hans Coper

Along with Leach, the other internationally renowned studio potters of mid-twentieth-century Britain are Lucie Rie (1902-1995) and Hans Coper (1920-1981). Their technically brilliant, austere and considered work could hardly be further removed from the rustic-oriental school. Rie and Coper were both émigrés – from Austria and Germany respectively – steeped in the modernist creed of Central Europe. They brought with them a refined approach to form coupled with a subtle use of colour and texture, which only gradually came to be appreciated.

When Rie arrived in London in 1938, she was already a prize-winning potter. At first she worked in earthenware, as she had in Vienna, then she was persuaded to try stoneware and porcelain, which admirably suited her delicate, precisely thrown pots. For most of her life she was interested only in the most basic shapes – vases and bowls – with the simplest decoration, either glaze or scratched lines. Her surfaces are often desiccated and pitted, with exquisitely thin walls. The pots' resonance lies in their simplicity, refinement and balance.

At the end of the Second World War Rie supported herself making ceramic buttons for the fashion world. Coper, who had escaped to England just before the war, joined her buttonmaking team in 1946. Though trained as a sculptor, painter and engineer, he decided to carry on working in clay, sharing Rie's workshop until 1958 and building up her confidence by his belief in her work. Rie's sgraffito decoration became a leitmotif of the 1950s. She began to produce tall, slender-necked vases to which she gave exaggerated flared lips and which she developed and refined over the next three or so decades.

Like Rie, Coper worked chiefly with a few simply thrown shapes. These he manipulated, compressed and flattened, often forging two or more into a single entity. Early on he used strict interlocking geometric shapes but gradually softened the transitions between them. He glazed each piece several times, building up a matt texture which he abraded until it became 'ancient' and worn-looking. Colour was limited to a light or a dark glaze. During the 1960s, his forms became more vertical, in 'spade pots' with squeezed

*above:* a plate decked with one of the Transport patterns designed by Eric Ravilious for Wedgwood in 1937; it was first produced 11 years after his death, in 1953, when a dinner set for six cost £17 3s. 6d. *right:* a stoneware cup form by Hans Coper, c. 1972, seemingly balanced on a single point – actually joined by a metal pin – and with a typically abraded surface; it is a precursor of his Cycladic arrowhead pots.

narrow mouths, and 'arrowhead' pots seemingly balancing on a single point (in fact joined by a metal pin); they were based on archaic forms such as cycladic figures, with a nod to Arp, Brancusi and Giacometti.

**Artist decorators**

The first ceramics to cause a stir internationally after the Second World War were by Pablo Picasso, who blended art and craft in a thoroughly modern manner. He learnt traditional potting methods from Suzanne Ramié at the Madoura pottery in Vallauris in the South of France in 1946-47, and went on to sculpt his own forms as well as exuberantly incising, painting and decorating ready-made ones. In the first of two years he created some 2,000 pieces. Their painting is recognisably by him: bold faces on plates; goats; bullfighting scenes; 'women' jugs. In a similar vein Jean Cocteau decorated a series of face plates. Post-war British artists who have painted on ceramics include Graham Sutherland, Patrick Caulfield and Bruce McLean.

While it is impossible to do justice to the multitude of inter-war European ceramicists – in France, Jean Luce's sunrays for Haviland spring to mind – the 1950s graphics of Pietro Fornasetti (1913-1988) are particularly enduring. (They were prefigured by the architect Gio Ponti's long-limbed figures in impossible de Chirico-like perspectives which he created on porcelain for Richard-Ginori from 1923 to 1930.) Fornasetti's mostly black-and-white graphic *tours de force*, still made today, combine traditional engraved images with surrealistic settings. Subjects include architectural teasets; musical instruments; and women's faces – some 500 different ones, as beads in a necklace, apples, balloons and light bulbs. In recent decades, members of the Memphis design group, in particular Matteo Thun, have raided Futurism and Constructivism to produce angular, gleaming ceramic forms.

**Scandinavia**

Finland's leading pottery company, Arabia (an offshoot of Rörstrand in Sweden), produced modernistic designs from the 1920s into the 1940s and 1950s. Finnish and

*right:* an area of bedroom calm dominated by a rough-surface stoneware piece by Colin Gorry (a visual effects designer at the BBC as well as a potter) standing tall above contemporary Japanese bowls on a sixteenth-century Japanese carrying-case bedside table. The painting is by Nancy Baldwin. *top left:* small vessels punctuated with taller vases; from left, a Japanese bowl, a Lucie Rie, three Mo Jupp beakers and an elegant Elizabeth Fritsch. *centre left:* a long-necked, balanced white Lucie Rie vessel stands out luminously beside a curvy-necked wooden duck and two rougher pots. *bottom left:* a parade of low-lying Lucie Rie bowls and a vase beneath a wall of drawings.

Swedish ceramic and glass wares were in demand – and imitated – throughout Europe, particularly in Britain. The most forward-looking Swedish company was Gustavsberg, where the influential designer Wilhelm Kåge (1889-1950) was art director from 1917 to 1949, followed by the much imitated Stig Lindberg. Rörstrand and the Upsala-Ekeby combine were other Swedish producers of the 'Contemporary' look.

## America

American modernist ceramics kicked off in the 1930s with the plain singing colours and freeform shapes of Frederick H. Rhead's Fiesta, made for 20 years from 1936 by Homer Laughlin in red, blue, green, yellow and ivory. It was designed to be mixed and matched; a cheaper version, Harlequin, was sold in Woolworth. Perhaps the most important range was Russel Wright's American Modern, made by the Steubenville Pottery from 1939 to 1959. It came in seven shades and curvy forms. Some 80 million pieces were sold, making it the most popular tableware ever. The other great American ceramic designer of the period was Eva Zeisel.

## Post-war Britain

From 1942 to August 1952, thanks to the Second World War and its aftermath, only plain white china was made in Britain for home consumption; decoration was banned. Once restrictions were lifted there was frantic demand for lively designs. While this was supplied in part by florals and other proven successes, bold new patterns followed derived from Scandinavian design, Festival of Britain graphics such as atom formations, and the US. Straight lines were eschewed for rounded, organic forms. Orange, turquoise, lime green and acid yellow were a piquant antidote to wartime drabness. The same colours and motifs appeared on textiles, wallpapers, carpets and ceramics alike.

In 1952 the ceramic designer Roy Midwinter travelled from Britain to Canada on a sales trip for his father's pottery firm, W.R.

left: a triangular Swedish serving board from Rörstrand's Picknick range (1956); its design, by Marianne Westman, has some similarities with the English firm Midwinter's Saladware, which was introduced in 1955. Riviera (right), 1954, was another Midwinter design, for their modernist Stylecraft range; Hugh Casson made the seven hand-tinted drawings for it on holiday in the South of France. Riviera proved extremely popular and was renamed Cannes when it was adapted to fit the Fashion shape in 1960, which did away with rims on plates. below: a late 1940s tin-glazed ewer by Stig Lindberg for Gustavsberg.

Midwinter. He was particularly struck by the ceramics of Eva Zeisel and Russel Wright. On his return home he began to develop his own modernist range, Stylecraft, which boasted 'quartic' plates – like a television screen. It was launched in February 1953 with 36 contemporary designs, most by Jessie Tait, and was an immediate bestseller. Some were hand-painted, others, like Hugh Casson's jaunty Riviera 'sketch' (made until the late 1970s) were printed, then hand-coloured.

A new shape, Fashion, with rimless coupé plates, was launched in 1955. Its six designs included one by the young Terence Conran who, the same year, co-designed Saladware with Roy Midwinter, inspired by a Fornasetti design of anthropomorphic vegetables. Other collectable Midwinter patterns range from Peter Scott's naturalistic Wild Geese (1955) to black-and-white striped Zambesi (1956) with red-lined jugs and handles. By the early 1960s, the Contemporary look had dated. In response, Midwinter introduced Fine in 1962, designed by David Queensberry (then Professor of Ceramics at the Royal College of Art) with Roy Midwinter. Fine boasted a cylindrical form reminiscent of eighteenth-century creamware and straight-sided cups. Decoration included wide rusty-hued stripes, large spots, and Jessie Tait's best-selling Spanish Garden which was inspired by a Liberty tie.

**Poole pottery**: Another keenly collected post-war British name is Poole – Carter, Stabler and Adams as its art pottery side was called from 1921. In the 1920s and 1930s, Truda Carter had made jagged and floral decorations on John Adams's shapes. However, by the end of the Second World War, with a scattered workforce and outmoded products, Poole decided to concentrate on industrially produced ceramics. Modern, fluid shapes were developed, including a distinctive waisted look. Poole blended avant-garde shapes (for example, Free Form, 1956) with traditional hand-throwing and hand-painting of semi-abstract designs in muted yellows, greys, greens and browns. In 1963 a separate design studio, based on the Arabia studio, was

181

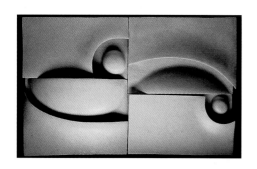

*previous page, left:* an elegant hanging cabinet allowing the display of many varied pieces. On top of it are bowls by David Leach, Norah Braden and Katharine Pleydell-Bouverie – who all trained with Bernard Leach. Next row a platter by Japanese National Treasure Tatsuzo Shimaoka and Dan Kelly, then two rows of fluted bowls by David Leach; beneath them are a contemporary Irish bowl and a jug by Takeshi Yasuda; bowls by Katharine Pleydell-Bouverie, John Bedding and David Leach and on the bottom row, one bowl by Jim Malone and two by William Marshall, who also worked with Bernard Leach; *right:* 1930s vases by Keith Murray for Wedgwood on an undulating table of 1948 by Neil Morris of the Glasgow firm H. Morris & Co.

introduced. Their chargers and plates are particularly striking – many in hot, clashing colours, with outlined patterns, and heavy sgraffito.

Hornsea and Rye were two other distinctive half-commercial, half-studio pottery post-war makers. Hornsea was founded in 1949, but began to make modern wares only when John Clappison arrived in 1958. Rye Pottery was refounded in 1947 by John and Walter Cole. It produced tin-glazed majolica inspired by seventeenth-century British and Moorish wares and decorated with modern stars (including Festival Star for the Festival of Britain in 1951), stripes and geometric motifs. Of other British lines, Meakin's Studio echoed Wright's American Modern, while Ridgway made the best-known 1950s plates of all: black-and-white Homemaker, sold through Woolworth, depicting contemporary furniture.

### America: mid-twentieth century

American ceramics underwent a revolutionary change in the 1950s, breaking free from their European past. Immediately after the Second World War, vigorously decorated ceramics by artists like Picasso, Miró and Luca Fontana stirred sensibilities away from neutral colours and polite forms, to the energetic surfaces of American Expressionist painting, to abstract decoration and asymmetry.

One of the chief catalysts for change was Peter Voulkos (born 1924). He started off making conventional oriental wares, but began to treat clay more freely after summer school at the experimental Black Mountain College, North Carolina in 1953. The following year he founded a ceramics department at Otis Art Institute, Los Angeles and worked with a group of like-minded students including Kenneth Price, Paul Soldner and John Mason.

There was no single style, but objects were assembled from separate elements (both thrown and modelled), while finishes were rough. Voulkos gave young potters the confidence to break rules. In 1959 he moved to the University of California, Berkeley, where Ron Nagle and Stephen DeStaebler were among his students. He continued to produce ever more fragmented, cracked, pierced pots with extraneous bits stuck on.

*left:* a wall piece by Ruth Duckworth, 1988. A stoneware mural she made for a bank in Chicago measures 7.3 metres (24 feet) long. *below:* this Rye pottery vase was exhibited at the Festival of Britain, 1951; its decoration was known as Festival Star.

**Funk and fetish**. The 1960s saw the emergence in the West Coast of the Funk movement. Its leader was Robert Arneson (born 1930), whose 'shocking' work was exhibited in art galleries. Strongly influenced by Dada and Surrealism, Arneson and others made casually modelled, virulently coloured everyday objects – as Claus Oldenburg was doing in soft materials – juxtaposing them with outrageous punning images: Arneson's Typewriter with nail-varnished fingers for keys, Fred Bauer's phallic cameras, David Gilhooly's frogs. Roy Lichtenstein made cup, teapot and head sculptures. Though hugely imitated funk had fizzled out by 1975.

At the same time a 'fetish finish' school had grown up, of trompe-l'oeil 'super-objects'. Their finest creator was Marilyn Levine, who turned out 'leather' suitcases, jackets and boots. Other popular clay disguisers were Richard Shaw who made 'cardboard' teasets and pipes, while Richard Notkin fashioned miniature skeleton cups and nuclear cooling-tower teapots.

Of more 'traditional' potters, Ruth Duckworth (born 1919) has moved even further than Hans Coper towards abstract sculpture by abandoning symmetry – previously the basis of all studio pottery. Her delicate, disturbing pots contain jagged rims and split volumes. Duckworth escaped to England from Nazi Germany in 1936. Her first clay pieces were stiff cylinder vases and modern tea and coffee services. She then began to make small, intimate porcelain vessels which sprouted wings and other growths as they became more organic and abstract. After teaching at Central School of Art in London for four years – where she had a liberating effect – in 1964 she left for the University of Chicago, to expand the scale of her work. She has lived and worked in America ever since.

The figurative tradition is also strong amongst American potters: Viola Frey's large figures, Robert Arneson's portrait busts and the anthropomorphic painted pots of Rudy Autio and Akio Takamori are some of the best-known examples. Of wackier, more allusive potters Adrian Saxe 'collages' symbolic figurative elements such as antelopes on to vessels, and 'quotes' from antique ceramics such as Sèvres (where he worked in the 1980s). A 1985 royal blue vessel stamped with a gold fleur-de-lis is crowned with a bomb – referring to the

Variations on a theme in the work of one ceramicist make an intriguing display when shown together. *left:* row upon row of irregular teabowls by Ewen Henderson, who mixes types of clay to achieve a volcanic-like texture; beneath them sit bowls by Gordon Baldwin, a seventeenth-century Sawankhalok piece and a square Oribe dish. A commanding pierced plate by the American ceramicist Peter Voulkos hangs alongside. *below left:* a wall of chunky angular vessels by Alison Britton looks imposingly sculptural and modern; on the table is 'Vessel in the form of a Voice' by Gordon Baldwin, 1983. *below right:* the surface decorations of the Brittons stand out distinctly close to and against the fine lines of the straw roof outside. *right:* two 'winged' vessels by Colin Pearson flanked by Dan Kelly pieces. On the bottom row, two forms by Ewen Henderson flank a Picasso plate, while the small bowl is by Chuck Schwartz.

French monarchy's greedy desire for Sèvres porcelain. The clever nature of his work has led to the term 'the smart pot'. Betty Woodman is another inventive potter who draws on ceramic history. Although hugely desirable, work by seminal twentieth-century American potters tends to be far more expensive and out of reach than its European equivalents.

### Post-war pottery in England – hand-built, organic and post-modern

England witnessed a similar if less dramatic shift away from thrown vessels to the hand-built. Among the potters who turned to sculptural forms was Gordon Baldwin (born 1932), whose enigmatic rounded and stretching shapes have scratched and drawn-on surfaces. During the 1960s he made shiny black pieces before shifting to white ones, at the same time moving to extreme versions of the vessel. Today he restricts himself to a palette of black, white and grey save for an intense sky blue. His most impressive works, the leaning, imperious, tapering Monads of the 1980s, are dirty-white with black markings; they make powerful assemblies when gathered together.

During the 1970s in England, a strand of organic ceramics got underway. One of the best 'organic' potters, Ewen Henderson, creates 'volcanic'-surfaced pots combining porcelain and stoneware, their subtle colours like seams of rock. Similar rough surfaces occur in the work of Sarah Radstone and the Spanish potter Claudi Casanovas, while Jennifer Lee builds up thin layers of coloured clays like a rock face. Gillian Lowndes, creator of wonderful kinky pipes, uses bubbling surfaces to encase found household objects. Organic imagery appears in Peter Simpson's intricate early work, reminiscent of fossils and upturned fungi, and in Mary Rogers' translucent, paper-thin pinched porcelain bowls suggesting petals or sea anenomes; Jacqueline Poncelet's equally delicate cast white bone-china bowls have a more man-made feel.

**New Ceramics**: Poncelet's work was part of the 'New Ceramics' movement among students tutored by Hans Coper at the Royal College of Art in the early 1970s – when earthenware and bright underglaze colours also underwent a resurgence. They included Elizabeth Fritsch, Alison Britton, Jill Crowley, Carol McNicoll and Glenys Barton. Fritsch's flattened forms are painted with three-dimensional floating cubes, giving them

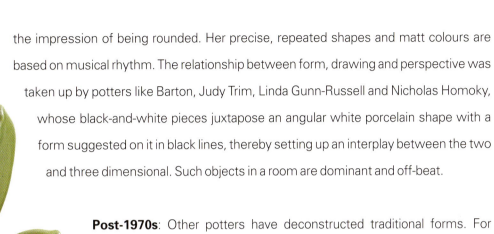

the impression of being rounded. Her precise, repeated shapes and matt colours are based on musical rhythm. The relationship between form, drawing and perspective was taken up by potters like Barton, Judy Trim, Linda Gunn-Russell and Nicholas Homoky, whose black-and-white pieces juxtapose an angular white porcelain shape with a form suggested on it in black lines, thereby setting up an interplay between the two and three dimensional. Such objects in a room are dominant and off-beat.

**Post-1970s**: Other potters have deconstructed traditional forms. For example, in the 1980s Martin Smith cast rich red earthenware bowls, and cut and assembled them into flatter geometric shapes which he painted. Idiosyncratic boxes containing a folk world of dwellings and animals were produced by Ian Godfrey; Grayson Perry makes vases collaged with messages about sex and gender, while a more complex satirist, and the gleaming opposite of organic, is Richard Slee. His super-shiny, electric-bright kitsch objects inventively play on ceramic history. An enemy of the notion of good taste, he has made a series based on the Toby jug. Any object by him in a domestic setting would look modern and intriguing.

### Contemporary hand-thrown pots

In the 1960s and 1970s, a new element of subversion was introduced to the British hand-thrown tradition. Colin Pearson, previously at Winchcombe, started to produce pots based on ancient Chinese bronzes to which he gave wings. Other modern wheel potters include Walter Keeler, John Ward, Joanna Constantinidis and Kenyan-born Magdalene Odundo, whose burnished pots draw on African and pre-Columbian pit-fired vessels. (The French potter Pierre Bayle also makes splendid burnished pots.) Her work gives the impression of being simple, ancient and modern at the same time. Janice Tchalenko is a popular and influential creator of domestic ware. In 1979 she began to experiment with high-fired, richly coloured painting of flowers, creating standard ware for Dart Pottery from the mid-1980s. Among the best of a host of younger British potters are Takeshi Yasuda, maker of Tang-inspired splashed wares, Julian Stair, Rupert Spira and Edmund de Waal.

*left:* the painstaking geometric decoration on many of Elizabeth Fritsch's pieces, such as this 'Optical' stoneware bottle vase, is influenced by musical rhythms; she also plays with perspectives, flattens her forms, and has claimed that her work operates in two and a half dimensions. *above:* earthenware Flower (1991) by Richard Slee whose work is characterised by bright, luscious glazes (most easily obtained with earthenware), bizarre forms, and inventive references to historic ceramics.

*left:* this ceramics paradise of a sitting room boasts large Gordon Baldwins in the foreground, bowls and vases by Bernard Leach the other end of the table, a handsome Magdalene Odundo on the fireplace and many pieces by Shoji Hamada on the shelves. The television shows a pot by Shiro Tsujimura – a real bowl by him sits under the anglepoise. *top:* skyward-pointing pieces by Gordon Baldwin on the bookcases and mantelpiece of a study; next to the one on the far right is a skull by Richard Notkin; in the centre hangs a Roger Hilton gouache. *above:* a dining-room display in which pieces of different sizes fit pleasingly into Habitat shelves including, top left, a pair of Betty Woodmans alongside a large Ewen Henderson and beneath it a Gordon Baldwin.

# clever decorating ideas

**novel and eye-catching ways to display your collection**

For far too long there has been an unspoken belief that the proper place for china is behind glass doors or set stolidly on a mantelpiece. This just is not true. Such limitations are stifling and dull: where is the aesthetic pleasure in something you can barely see (thanks to glazing), or a stale decorating cliché? The eye needs to be surprised and refreshed. As indeed it can be, with really very little effort or cost.

The china illustrated in this chapter is not necessarily fine or rare. What is striking is the effect to which it has been put: massed together, creating textural 'wallpaper', drawing the eye to a high ledge, to determine the colour scheme of a room, or simply for exuberant, decorative fun. This was, after all, how porcelain in Europe started out – as a glorified theatrical device. In crazily crammed porcelain rooms at the turn of the eighteenth century, walls were alive with busily choreographed rows of vases perched on wall brackets, above doors, across shelves and set in niches.

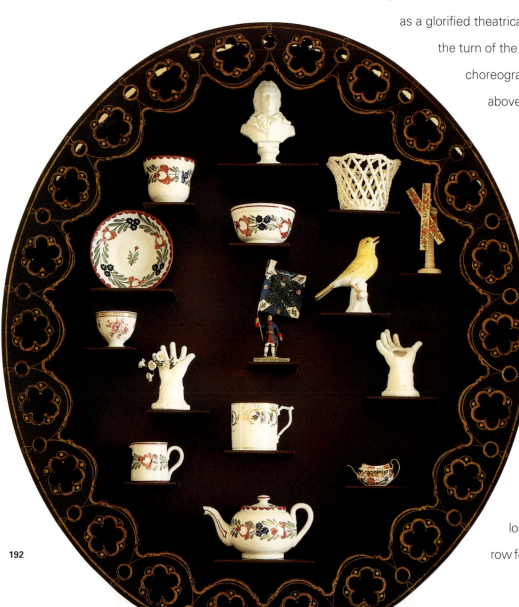

This principle still holds good, as modern interpretations demonstrate, employing mostly functional ceramics to purely decorative effect. For those unwilling or unable to line an entire room with china, it is possible to use a small area – above a fireplace or loo – to bold effect. Indeed, the smaller the space you inhabit the more essential it is not simply to fill but to use it inventively.

The extremities of a room respond well to the titivating effect of china. They have no obvious other use. A few jugs or teacups provide points of interest, happy events for the eye. The long thin rectangle of wall above a door is too narrow for most paintings, but the ideal hanging ground for a row of plates. Should you feel a minimalist streak coming on, plump for a single strong shape: a large vase atop a wardrobe, for example, or a meat dish above a window.

## China on walls

**Plates**: Often a plate's decoration can best be seen when it is hung on a wall, like a mini painting. Since even the largest platter is small compared to the standard picture, there should be room for several at once, and for composing in geometric shapes – diamonds, squares or circles. Creating neat patterns makes particular sense in panelled rooms, where walls are already divided into framing devices: even one plate per panel looks chic. Massed plates create an impressive sense of order. A vertical row down the side of a bookcase or between two windows makes a smart and eye-catching march. Individual pieces do not have to be of great interest; what is necessary are similar designs or colours and, for added interest, a contrasting background – bold stripes positively invite china. Plates of several sizes add variety and scale.

Cramped areas, such as passages or staircases, enable china to be seen close up – unlike a watercolour or photograph, no glass is needed to protect it from light and dirt. In exuberant nineteenth-century style Victor Hugo arranged plates on the ceiling as well as the walls of his house at St Peter Port, Guernsey. The house is now a museum, and the upside-down china makes a startling sight. A room in the Santos Palace in Lisbon also boasts plates on the ceiling – this time late Ming blue-and-white.

**Brackets**: For objects that do not sit flat against a wall, brackets are the answer. Ceramics should be positioned for bold theatrical effect rather than where a shelf happens to be. When displayed prominently, even conventional *objets d'art* look precious and punchy. A chipped agateware vase will stand out as handsomely as an exquisite figure. A bracket can also become part of another composition – above a tablescape, or surrounded by plates on a wall. Brackets arranged in a geometric pattern, flanking a picture, or running down the sides of a door in the style of William and Mary's decorator, Daniel Marot, are always strking. An ascending triangle of brackets above a fireplace – a device Horace Walpole used in his china closet at Strawberry Hill – looks stark and dramatic.

*left:* a jaunty collection of English and Continental china collected over the years by the writer June Ducas and shown to intriguing effect on a hanging shelf of her own design. Although of diverse shapes, the pale-hued pieces are unified by their display on a dark background, and each one stands out strongly.

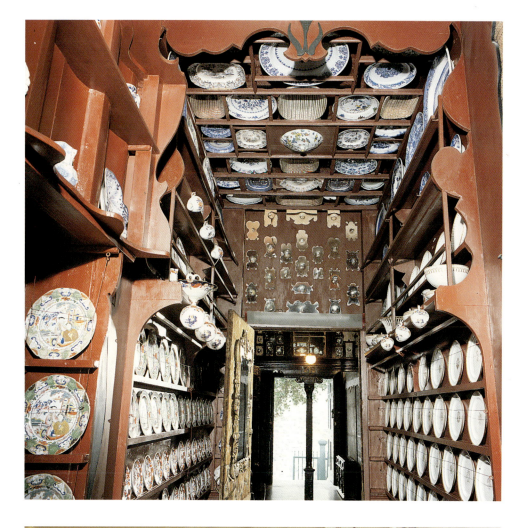

*left:* the patchwork of plates in the porcelain passage at Hauteville House, Victor Hugo's home in St Peter Port, Guernsey from 1856 to 1870 (when he also designed the room overleaf) extends even to the ceiling; lining the walls is the Sèvres dinner service given to the poet by the king in 1825. *right:* the porcelain closet at Newhailes, East Lothian was decorated in 1824 by the architect William Burn; its Italian maiolica, seventeenth- and eighteenth-century Chinese blue-and-white and Kakiemon and European wares are elegantly displayed on myriad special little shelves. *below left:* the plates marching down mirrors in and around this bathroom show the possibilities of creating a striking wall-to-wall effect in a humbler setting; few of the plates match, but all boast a pinkish floral decoration. It is an effective way of hanging pretty but not particularly distinctive china.

*previous pages:* a decor of plates and painted panels designed by Victor Hugo – originally as two rooms – for his mistress Juliette Drouet, who followed him into exile in Guernsey and lived at a house known as Hauteville Fairy; it was recreated at the Victor Hugo museum in Paris when it opened in 1903. In it, the pattern of the splendidly regimented plates is more important than the individual items, which are an amalgam of different styles. *this page:* the blue-and-white lidded vase at Chateau Malleret in the Médoc (*above*) looks particularly good against a red background; *right:* oriental vases climbing a 'tree' at Schloss Wörlitz, near Dessau, in the Chinese rooms decorated in the taste of Sir William Chambers; *far right:* a sequence of small eighteenth-century vases from the Nanking Cargo (salvaged in 1984) on one of two panels flanking a fireplace at Glamis Castle; the brackets were designed by Melissa Wyndham.

### Shelves

Erecting a shelf is the simplest decorative decision: technically straightforward, yet custom-built; it can also easily be moved around. Most allow a display several objects deep, with large items as background and bibelots in front. For a dramatic show, position two or more tiers above a fireplace. Disparate objects look good on small hanging shelves. The shelves themselves need not come in conventional shape. Freestanding obelisk shelves are a popular decorators' device used by the inventive David Hicks (in chunky versions) and by Nancy Lancaster of Colefax & Fowler. One object can be placed on each shelf – the eye automatically moves from top to bottom.

A secure way of balancing plates or tiles is on shelves with ridges in them. These are neat and narrow and therefore useful in small spaces or on stairwells. For those of magpie disposition, a motley assortment of plates can be hung up and used, rather than stacked in cupboards. The other way of displaying useful wares is on dressers – that popular and crowded piece of kitchen furniture in which the English take particular pleasure.

### Games with scale and colour

Some of the simplest and most decorative effects can be created by playing with scale and colour. Large jars in a small room look unexpectedly grand (on a not-so-small scale, Elton John has an dramatic wall of shelves filled with outsize china jars) while lining up exquisite tea bowls on a tall, heavy mantelpiece emphasises their delicacy.

Similarly, setting china against bold colours accentuates its own hues: blue-and-white gleams inkily against cardinal red walls; creamware sits silky and snowy in a dark wood niche. Even the colour of a shelf's edge points up what it contains. If the china possesses strong colouring, let it dictate the background colour of its niche – or even the whole room: dusty pink for black-and-white Fornasetti, perhaps, or pale blue for vivid pink lustre.

In other words, when deciding how to display your china be bold and imaginative. You have nothing to lose. Ceramics are superbly portable. If you don't like one arrangement – and even if you do – you can always make another.

right: the breakfast room in a Welsh home. Its pretty floral porcelain – mostly English, including Derby and Coalport – was bought in stages from Portobello Market in London; the faux panelling is painted in a soothing Farrow & Ball National Trust colour which complements the pretty pink flowers on the china, the tablecloth and the upholstery. above: the cool wide passage between the kitchen and the breakfast room is hung with equally airy, widely spaced blue-and-white transfer ware.

*above:* Maurice Ravel arranged his dining room himself, placing the nineteenth-century Chinese porcelain in a two-tier display on a deep-fringed shawl; today the house in the Ile de France is a museum. *right:* in Carl Larsson's 1890s dining-room decor at Sundborn in Sweden, china is displayed on a high shelf picked out in the same red as the chairs, in contrast to the green skirting and cream wall. *far right:* shelves painted a contrasting colour to the wall and lined with patterned material enhance the display of modern and antique Swiss Thun ware in the home of Mary Wondrausch; south Devon jugs of c. 1920 hang under them, beneath which is a twentieth-century Spanish plate.

*right:* the fine pinstripes and curious biomorphic forms of these black-and-white 1970s Japanese flower-arranging vases are enhanced by the graphic lines of grey-and-white wallpaper coming together from different angles on the stairwell. They were collected by textile designer Sue Timney of Timney-Fowler – itself renowned for black-and-white designs – as were the motley pots *above*, whose arrangement in her home on a shelf below eye level draws attention to their varied patterns rather than to their forms.

Even a few plates can have a dramatic impact when set against a richly coloured wall – especially if marshalled into a disarming pattern. *far left:* unusual square armorial plates, themselves hung as a square, benefit from being placed close to where a green wall turns into yellow. *left:* a vertical march of nineteenth-century Paris animal plates against a sunny orange background. *right:* a pretty arrangement of simply decorated Meissen porcelain in a smoky blue niche at Quay House in Clifden, Connemara, a delightful bed and breakfast.

*previous pages, main picture:* a handsome Victorian sideboard in the home of the textile designer Sue Timney, packed high and tight with her collection of bright, geometric-decorated 1960s vases; at the other end of the room (*above right*) is an ebonised cabinet by Anthony Collett, decked on high and at floor level with contemporary glass and ceramics, and alongside it (*below right*) tall Arts and Crafts jugs and modern French vases sit on a Victorian fireplace. *this page, right:* a Liberty fireplace in Sue Timney's library contains an array of ceramics in earth colours, as does the high ledge above it which carries all the way round the room; *below left:* the view from the fireplace in the same room, with a collection of 1950s and 1960s ceramics on an Arts and Crafts oak cabinet; *above left:* yellow plates from Marrakesh line the uppermost reaches of designer Anthony Collett's kitchen, injecting a bright hue into the warm rich marbled interior; the smaller painted plates are from Samos.

Ceramics with strong profiles or lacy composition look striking in a strong light, and therefore on and against glass. *left:* intricate Sainte Radegonde ceramics, named after the small Touraine village where they were made – the secret of their 'noodle' construction is now lost. *right:* ten brown bottles stand in silhouette against a window in the Anvers house of Belgian architect Vincent van Duysen, looking like an installation; chunky ceramic vessels fill the foreground.

# care & repair

**how to look after your collection**

## Do

Always treat ceramics with respect, as they can easily chip or crack if knocked or banged down on a surface

Hold a piece with both hands, supporting the base where possible; remove any lid or loose base before picking up

Keep restored ceramics out of direct sunlight and away from smoke, as these can discolour restoration work

When transporting ceramics wrap each piece separately (including lids) in plenty of packaging so that items do not touch. Stand plates on their rims, in order to absorb shock better if knocked

When unpacking allow lots of space, and take care not to knock anything newly unwrapped. Check all packaging before throwing it out

Ask a dealer if you may handle his stock before helping yourself

## Don't

Don't pick objects up by their weak points: handles, spouts, or top edges, as these may be restored or cracked

Try to avoid stacking plates as the weight can cause cracks and the foot rims grind small scratches into the plate underneath. If you have to stack, place padding between each plate

Don't apply self-adhesive stickers or sellotape to ceramics, as these can stain or lift off glazes and gilding

Try to avoid using plate springs to hang plates on the wall, as the increased tension can cause cracks; far better are adjustable transparent acrylic hangers. However, if you do decide on plate springs, use modern, plastic-covered ones and take care to choose the correct size

## Cleaning

Ceramics on display will need washing from time to time. Before starting, check that each item has no restoration work as, being unfired, this will wash off in warm water. If there are signs of restoration, just wipe the piece with a damp cloth, using no detergent

To wash a ceramic you need a draining board, a dry towel, a fine paint brush, warm water and mild washing-up detergent

Place the piece in the sink, wash gently with water and detergent, and use the brush to clean any small corners. Allow to drip dry on the towel on a clear draining board

To remove stains soak the piece in a stain-removing powder such as Biotex (following the dilution instructions on the packet). Again, soaking is not suitable for restored pieces or for low-fired ceramics

Never soak ceramics in bleach, as this will damage the body and cause gold decoration to bleed across the china. It could also cause a fur-like covering to grow on the china

The build-up of crystals that causes rings of stains under plant-pots can be removed by soaking the piece in a water softener (for example, calgon) and/or stain-removing powder – or both together

## Damaged ceramics

Damaged china is considerably less valuable than perfect china – often only a third (or less) of a similar perfect piece. (This also means that if you can put up with the odd crack, chip or breakage, you can afford examples of china normally out of your price range.) One exception is delftware, which chips so easily there are few perfect examples, and the price is unaffected by minor damage

Get to know likely places where chips and cracks may appear, such as spouts of jugs and teapots, handles on cups, all extremities on figures

Damage on figures is graded, for example a broken head affects the value far more than a lost finger or chipped bocage

## How to check for restoration work

Restored areas of china may discolour with age; look closely and you may be able to see colour variation on a restored area

If in doubt, check with an ultra-violet lamp. The restored area will appear a different colour when exposed to ultra-violet rays (which will not damage ceramics)

If you gently prick the suspected area with a pin, the softer restored glue and paint can be felt

Gently tapping a piece will make it ring; if the item is cracked it will make a dull ping

## Repair

Remember that restoration work can be expensive as it is very time-consuming

Restoration will never reinstate the value of a broken piece, but it will make it look better

Take care to secure references before leaving your precious pieces with a restorer, or to check out other repairs undertaken by them

Many ceramic dealers offer a restoration service; local museums and auction houses are also worth approaching for advice

Restoration is not suitable for items that are used, for example plates and tureens, as the glue will melt when heated or washed

# glossary
## the meaning of ceramic terms

**barbotine** method of painting pottery using coloured slips; popular in late nineteenth century America

**biscuit** pottery or porcelain fired once and left unglazed

**bocage** modelled ceramic flowers and foliage used as a background or support to figures, especially in eighteenth-century England

**body** the material from which earthenware, stoneware or porcelain is made; with porcelain the body is often called 'paste'

**bone china** a pure-white porcelain containing bone ash as well as petuntse and kaolin; the dominant English porcelain from the 1790s

**celadon** a chalky green, semi-translucent glaze found on Chinese stonewares

**china clay** *see* kaolin

**china stone** *see* petuntse

**Chinese export porcelain** porcelain made and decorated in China to European taste and designs, particularly in the seventeenth and eighteenth century

**chinoiserie** fanciful European decoration inspired by Chinese motifs; in high fashion during the eighteenth century

**cloisonné** a design on metal of wire outlines filled with coloured enamels; the effect was mimicked on nineteenth-century china

**cobalt** mineral used to create the colour blue on ceramics

**creamware** a cream-coloured, lead-glazed earthenware body developed c. 1760 by Josiah Wedgwood; it is tougher and finer than tin-glazed earthenware. Also called 'Queen's ware' after a creamware tea service commissioned by Queen Charlotte

**delftware** tin-glazed earthenware made at Delft in Holland and in England

**earthenware** porous pottery body, fired at under approximately 1000°C (1830°F) and therefore not vitrified (unlike stoneware)

**enamel colour** paint made from mid-eighteenth century from powdered glass and metallic oxides, allowing a wide range of colours; applied over the glaze, with which it fuses at a low temperature

**faience** French, German and Scandinavian name for tin-glazed earthenware

**famille rose, famille verte** Chinese porcelain decorated with predominantly pink or green enamel colours

**firing** the method whereby clay is turned into ceramic, through heat (usually in a kiln)

**flambé** crimson copper (reduction) glaze streaked with blue; first developed in China during the Sung dynasty (960-1280AD)

**flatbacks** Staffordshire figures with a flat, undecorated back, designed to stand on a fireplace

**garniture de cheminée** a set of three, five or seven vases to decorate a chimney piece, most commonly three lidded baluster shapes and two flared beakers

**glaze** a glassy coating applied to ceramics, making them watertight after firing; can be coloured or transparent, as in lead glaze

**grand feu** the French term for high-temperature colours

**hard-paste** 'true' porcelain made from kaolin and petuntse; it requires high firing (1300-1400°C/2370-2550°F) in order to vitrify

**incising** decoration scratched into a pot's surface

**ironstone** a hard white stoneware, or stone china, imitating porcelain, allegedly containing iron slag; popular from the early nineteenth century for dinner services

**Kakiemon** an asymmetric style of porcelain decoration based on that of the Japanese Kakiemon potting dynasty, in which large spaces are left white and the palette contains iron-red, bluey-green, yellow and pale blue; Kakiemon porcelain appeared in Europe in the late seventeenth century and was much imitated

**kaolin** a fine white feldspathic (crystalline) china clay; with petuntse, one of the essential ingredients of hard-paste porcelain

**kraak ware** late Ming blue-and-white porcelain with 8-12 radial panels and a central scene; imported to Europe in the seventeenth century

**kwaart** a transparent lead glaze applied to Dutch Delftware after firing to give the glossy sheen of oriental porcelain

**lambrequin** a baroque border pattern of drapery and scrollwork painted on ceramics, chiefly eighteenth-century French faience

**lustreware** pottery decorated with metallic paints and fired in a kiln starved of oxygen

**maiolica** tin-glazed earthenware painted with overglaze colours

**majolica** usually moulded earthenware decorated with strong-coloured lead glazes; first used as a trade name by Minton c. 1850

**mochaware** pottery with dendritic markings, often on coloured bands; made chiefly in England in the late eighteenth and nineteenth century

**overglaze** painting or transfer-printing applied after glazing

**parian** a white unglazed biscuit porcelain popular for statuary in the nineteenth century

**paste** the material from which porcelain is made

**pearlware** a bluish-white earthenware introduced by Josiah Wedgwood in 1779; it became even more popular than creamware

**petit feu** the French name for low-temperature or enamel colours – far more varied than the high-temperature variety

**petuntse** also called china stone; a feldspathic (crystalline) rock essential in the production of hard-paste porcelain, which fuses into a kind of glass at an extremely high temperature (about 1450°C/2640°F)

**porcelain** a hard, translucent ceramic body, usually white and glazed. In Europe, hard-paste, soft-paste and bone china are variants

**pottery** sometimes used as a generic term for all ceramics, but more often refers to ceramics that are not porcelain – that is, earthenware and stoneware

**Prattware** late eighteenth- and early nineteenth-century relief-moulded earthenware with distinctive high-glazed palette dulled blue, ochre, and green – used originally by the Pratt family of Fenton

**press-moulding** a method of casting a vessel by pressing clay into a hollow mould

**raku** low-fired, lead-glazed Japanese pottery reduction glaze – whereby the oxygen in the kiln is kept to a minimum to encourage special colours from oxides and glazes

**salt-glaze** a pitted stoneware glaze obtained by throwing salt into the kiln during firing at a high temperature

**sang de boeuf** (French for ox blood) copper-red glaze with dark patches, developed in the Qing dynasty 1644-1912 (*see flambé*)

**sgraffito** decoration scratched through a layer of slip on a pot's surface

**slip** liquid mixture of clay and water used for decoration

**slipware** earthenware decorated with coloured slips

**soft-paste** an eighteenth-century alternative to hard-paste made in France and England, fired at a lower temperature (1100-1150°C/2010-2100°F) and made with frit (powdered glass) instead of petuntse in an attempt to create true porcelain before its composition was known; less easy to model than hard-paste

**sprigging** moulded relief decoration applied to a pot's surface (for example, jasperware)

**spongeware** pottery decorated by dabbing it with a sponge soaked in colour

**stoneware** a high-fired clay body (above 1150-1200°C/2100-2190°F), which is vitrified and therefore non-porous

**tin glaze** opaque white earthenware glaze made using tin oxide; maiolica, faience and delft are all tin-glazed ware

**transfer-printing** printed decoration transferred from a copperplate engraving via transfer paper on to ceramics

**underglaze** decoration applied before the glaze and final firing

**vitrified** when the glaze and body of an object fuse together, making it waterproof, after firing at a high temperature

# further reading

## recommended bibliography

### Useful sources

Reference Works, 'The Ceramic Book Specialists', 12 Commercial Road, Swanage, Dorset BH19 1DF (01929 424 423/fax 422 597); out-of-print books, exhibition and sale catalogues

Nicholas Merchant (01937 591 022/fax 591 033); tailor-made mail-order ceramics lists

Potterton Books (01845 501 218); mail-order

### General

Battie, David (Ed.), *Sotheby's Concise Encyclopedia of Porcelain* (Conran Octopus 1990). A good general guide

Caiger-Smith, Alan, *Tin Glaze Pottery in Europe and the Islamic World* (Faber & Faber 1973)

Charleston, Robert J. (Ed.), *World Ceramics* (Hamlyn 1968). Huge, splendid and truly international

Clark, Garth, *The Potter's Art: A Complete History of Pottery in Britain* (Phaidon 1995). Impressive and attractive

Cooper, Emmanuel, *A History of World Pottery* (Batsford, third edn 1988). Interestingly broad survey

Fleming, John and Honour, Hugh, *The Penguin Dictionary of Decorative Arts* (Viking Penguin 1989). Excellent entries on ceramic factories and figures

Godden, Geoffrey, *British Pottery* (Barrie & Jenkins 1974). Well-illustrated short chapters

Haggar, Reginald G. and Mankowitz, Wolf, *The Concise Encyclopedia of English Pottery and Porcelain* (André Deutsch 1957)

Hillier, Bevis, *Pottery and Porcelain 1700-1914* (Weidenfeld & Nicolson, 1968). Packed with stories, erudite and entertaining

Honey, W.B., *English Pottery & Porcelain* (A & C Black, sixth edn 1969). Old-fashioned and readable history from the middle ages to the nineteenth century

Lewis, Griselda, *A Collector's History of English Pottery* (Studio Vista 1969). Engaging and attractively illustrated

Gleeson, Janet (Ed.), *Miller's Collecting Pottery & Porcelain*,(Reed International 1997). Copiously illustrated short entries with price guides

Morley-Fletcher, Hugo (Ed.), *Techniques of the World's Great Masters of Pottery and Ceramics* (Phaidon/Christie's 1984). Well-written essays, excellent pictures

Sandon, John, *The Phillips Guide to English Porcelain of the 18th and 19th Centuries* (Merehurst 1989). An appealing read

Savage, George, *Eighteenth-century English Porcelain* (Spring Books 1964); *Seventeenth and Eighteenth-century French Porcelain* (Barrie & Rockcliff 1960); *Eighteenth-century German Porcelain* (Spring Books 1958, second edn 1962)

Savage, George and Newman, Harold, *An Illustrated Dictionary of Ceramics* (Thames & Hudson 1974, reprint 1989). Useful reference book

Schreiber, Charlotte, *Lady Charlotte Schreiber: extracts from her journal 1853-1891* (John Murray 1952). The passion of collecting

Somers Cocks, Anna, 'The Nonfunctional Use of Ceramics in the English Country House During the Eighteenth Century' in *The Fashioning and Functioning of the British Country House*, Gervaise Jackson-Stops and others (Eds) (National Gallery of Washington 1989)

### Blue and White

Archer, Michael, *Delftware: the tin-glazed earthenware of the British Isles* (HMSO 1997)

Atterbury, Paul, *Cornish Ware* (Richard Dennis 1996)

Copeland, Robert, *Spode's Willow Pattern* (Studio Vista/Christie's 1980)

Coysh, A.W. and Henrywood, R.K., *The Dictionary of Blue and White Printed Pottery 1780-1880* (Antique Collectors' Club 1982)

Fisher, Stanley W., *English Blue and White Porcelain of the 18th Century* (first edn Batsford 1947, reprint Fitzhouse 1989)

Fourest, Henry Pierre, *Delftware faience* (Thames & Hudson 1980)

Garner, Sir Harry, *Oriental Blue and White* (Faber & Faber 1954; third edn 1970)

Lambourne, Lionel, *The Aesthetic Movement* (Phaidon 1996). Intriguing account of the fashion for 'blue'

Macintosh, Duncan, *Chinese Blue and White*

*Porcelain* (Antique Collectors' Club 1977, third edn 1994)

Tippett, Paul, *Christie's Collectables: Blue and White China* (Little,Brown & Co 1997)

Watney, Bernard, *English Blue and White Porcelain of the 18th Century* (Faber & Faber, second edn 1973)

### Botanical

Adams, E., *Chelsea Porcelain* (Barrie & Jenkins 1987)

Aslin, Elisabeth and Atterbury, Paul, *Minton 1798-1910* (Victoria & Albert Museum 1976)

Austin, John C., *Chelsea Porcelain at Williamsburg* (Colonial Williamsburg Foundation 1977)

Bergesen, Victoria, *Majolica – British, Continental and American Wares* (Barrie & Jenkins 1989)

Cecil, Victoria, *Minton 'Majolica'* (Jeremy Cooper 1982)

Davies, P.H. and Rankine, R., *Wemyss Ware: A Decorative Scottish Pottery* (Scottish Academic 1986)

Lane, Arthur, *French Faience* (Faber & Faber 1963)

Mackenna, F.S., *Chelsea Porcelain Triangle and Raised Anchor Wares* (F. Lewis 1948)

Morley Fletcher, Hugo, *Meissen* (Barrie & Jenkins 1971)

Murdoch, John and Twitchett, John, *Painters and the Derby China Works* (exhibition catalogue, Victoria & Albert Museum 1987)

Rontgen, Robert E., *The Book of Meissen* (Schiffer 1986)

Snyder, Jeffrey B., and Bockol, Leslie, *Majolica: American & European Wares* (Schiffer 1994)

### Colours and shapes

Emmerson, Robin, *British Tea Pots and Tea Drinking* (HMSO 1992)

Godden, Geoffrey and Gibson, Michael, *Collecting Lustre Ware* (Barrie & Jenkins 1991)

Henrywood, R.K., *Relief-moulded Jugs 1820–1900* (Antique Collectors' Club 1984)

Miller, Phillip and Berthoud, M., *An Anthology of British Teapots* (Micawber 1985)

Street-Porter, Janet and Tim, *The British Tea Pot* (Angus & Robertson 1981)

Towner, Donald, *Creamware* (Faber & Faber 1978)

## Rustic
Haggar, Reginald G., *English Country Pottery* (Phoenix House 1950)

Lahaussois, Christine and Pannequin, Béatrice, *Terres Vernissées* (Editions Massin 1996)

Scheibli, Alain and Isabelle, *Faïences et Poteries Provençales* (Editions Scheibli 1996)

Slesin, Suzanne, Rozensztroch, Daniel and Cliff, Stafford, *Kitchen Ceramics* (Abbeville Press 1997)

Wondrausch, Mary, *Mary Wondrausch on Slipware* (A & C Black 1986)

## Figures and animals
Atterbury, Paul (Ed.), *The Parian Phenomenon* (Richard Dennis 1989)

Bradshaw, Peter, *18th Century Porcelain Figures* (Antique Collectors' Club 1981)

Haggar, R.G., *Staffordshire Chimney Ornaments* (Phoenix House 1955)

Honey, W.B., *Dresden China* (A & C Black 1934)

Lane, Arthur, *English Porcelain Figures of the 18th Century* (Faber & Faber 1961)

Oliver, Anthony, *The Victorian Staffordshire Figure* (St Martin's Press, New York 1971)

Rice, D.G., *English Porcelain Animals of the 19th Century* (Antique Collectors' Club 1989)

## Artist Potters
Richard Dennis Publications, 01460 240 044/fax 242 009, publishes individual volumes on many artist potters and nineteenth- and twentieth-century factories

Atterbury, Paul, *Ruskin Pottery* (Baxendale Press 1993); *William Moorcroft* (Richard Dennis 1989)

Coysh, A.W., *British Art Pottery* (David & Charles 1976)

Cross, A.J., *Pilkington's Royal Lancastrian Pottery and Tiles* (Richard Dennis 1980)

Dawson, Aileen, *Bernard Moore* (Richard Dennis 1982)

Dennis, Richard, *Doulton Stoneware and Terracotta 1870-1925* (Richard Dennis 1971); *Doulton Pottery from the Lambeth and Burslem Studios* (Richard Dennis 1975)

Greenwood, Martin, *The Designs of William De Morgan* (Richard Dennis 1989)

Halén, Widar, *Christopher Dresser* (Phaidon/Christie's 1990)

Haslam, Malcolm, *English Art Pottery 1865-1915* (Antique Collectors' Club 1975); *The Martin Brothers* (Richard Dennis 1978); *Elton Ware* (Richard Dennis 1989)

Jewitt, L., *Ceramic Art of Great Britain 1800-1900* (first edn 1878; revised by G. Godden, Barrie & Jenkins 1972)

Lyons, Harry, *Christopher Dresser* (New Century 1999)

Wakefield, Hugh, *Victorian Pottery* (Herbert Jenkins 1962)

## Modern
Batkin, Maureen, *Wedgwood Ceramics 1846-1959* (Richard Dennis 1982)

Clark, Garth, *American Ceramics 1876 to the Present* (Booth-Clibborn Editions 1987); Clark, Garth and Hughto, Margie, *A Century of Ceramics in the United States 1878-1978* (E.P. Dutton 1979)

Dormer, Peter, *The New Ceramics* (Thames & Hudson 1986)

Eatwell, A., *Susie Cooper Productions* (Victoria & Albert Museum 1987)

Hannah, Frances, *Ceramics: 20th Century Design* (Bell & Hyman 1986)

Hay, Jane, *Christie's Collectables: Art Deco Ceramics* (Little, Brown & Co 1996)

Hayward, Leslie, *Poole Pottery 1873-1995*, Paul Atterbury (Ed.) (Richard Dennis 1995)

Hill, Susan, *The Shelley Style: a collector's guide* (Jazz Publications 1990)

Jenkins, Steven, *Midwinter Pottery: A Revolution in British Tableware* (Richard Dennis 1997)

Lane, Peter, *Studio Ceramics* (Collins 1983)

Leach, Bernard, *A Potter's Book* (first edn 1940; Faber & Faber, third edn 1976)

Lynn, Martha Drexler, *Clay Today: A Catalogue of the Howard and Gwen Laurie Smits Collection at the Los Angeles County Museum of Art* (Chronicle Books, San Francisco 1990)

McCready, Karen, *Art Deco and Modernist Ceramics* (Thames & Hudson 1995)

Opie, J., *Scandinavia – Ceramics and Glass in the Twentieth Century* (Victoria & Albert Museum 1989)

Préaud, Tamara and Gauthier, Serge, *Ceramics of the Twentieth Century* (Phaidon 1982)

Spours, Judy, *Art Deco Tableware* (Ward Lock 1988)

Watson, Howard, *Collecting Clarice Cliff* (KF Publishing 1988); *The Colourful World of Clarice Cliff* (KF Publishing 1992)

Watson, Oliver, *British Studio Pottery: the Victoria and Albert Museum Collection* (Phaidon/Christie's 1990)

Wingfield Digby, George, *The Work of the Modern Potter in England* (John Murray 1952)

## Magazines
*American Ceramics*, 9 East 45th Street, New York, NY 10017 (001 212 661 4397)

*Ceramics: art and perception*, 35 Williams Street, Paddington, NSW 2021 (61 293 615 286/5402 fax). ceramicart@clinipath.com.au. Very good Australian magazine

*Ceramic Review*, 21 Carnaby Street, London W1V 1PH (0171 439 3377). Excellent bi-monthly English magazine

*Ceramics Monthly* (001 614 523 1660). American publication

*Studio Pottery* (01392 430 082). www.ceramic-society.co.uk. Good English quarterly

# where to buy

**shops and dealers with decorative stock at all prices**

## UK
### Pre mid-nineteenth century

Albert Amor, 37 Bury Street, London SW1Y 6AU (0171 930 2444). Eighteenth-century English porcelain

Gary Atkins, 107 Kensington Church Street, London W8 7LN (0171 727 8737). Attractive delftware, seventeenth- and eighteenth-century pottery, creamware, salt-glaze

Aurea Carter, Burton's Arcade, 296 Westbourne Grove, London W11 2PS (0171 731 3486). Eighteenth- and early nineteenth-century pottery and porcelain, including botanical and creamware

Andrew Dando, 4 Wood Street, Queen Square, Bath BA1 2JQ (01225 22702). Eighteenth- and nineteenth-century English pottery and porcelain

Jonathan Horne, 66c Kensington Church Street, London W8 4BY (0171 221 5658). Appealing delftware, creamware and pre-eighteenth century English pottery

Roderick Jellicoe, 114 Kensington Church Street, London W8 4BH (0171 727 7995). Decorative eighteenth-century porcelain

E. & H. Manners, 66a Kensington Church Street, London W8 4BY. English and Continental eighteenth-century ceramics

Mercury Antiques, 1 Ladbroke Road, London W11 3PA (0171 727 5106). Eighteenth- and early nineteenth-century English porcelain

Kevin Page Oriental Art, 2/6 Camden Passage, London N1 8ED (0171 226 8558). Chinese and Japanese porcelain up to the nineteenth century

Daphne Rankin & Ian Conn, 608 King's Road, London SW6 2DX (0171 384 1847). Seventeenth- to nineteenth-century Chinese and Japanese, plus Delft and Samson

Adrian Sassoon, London (0171 581 9888). Eighteenth-century Vincennes and Sèvres porcelain, and British studio ceramics

Spink & Son, 5 King Street, London SW1Y 6QS (0171 930 7888). Oriental ceramics; from the Neolithic period to the nineteenth century

Stockspring Antiques, 114 Kensington Church Street, London W8 4BH (0171 727 7995). Eighteenth- and nineteenth-century decorative porcelain, including blue-and-white, figures and floral

### Mid-nineteenth century to modern

Art Deco Etc, 73 Upper Gloucester Road, Brighton BN1 3LQ (01273 329 268). Victorian to 1970s, Poole a speciality

Beverley, 30 Church Street, London NW8 8EP (0171 262 1576). Art Nouveau and Art Deco

Britannia, Gray's Market, 58 Davies Street, London W1Y 2LP (0171 629 6772). Majolica

David Brower, 113 Kensington Church Street, London W8 7LN (0171 221 4155). European, oriental and English porcelain

Richard Dennis, 144 Kensington Church Street, London W8 4BN (0171 727 2061). English pottery from 1850 to 1950s/60s; Cornish Ware, Poole, Midwinter and contemporary potters

The Dining Room Shop, 62 White Hart Lane, London SW13 0PZ (0181 878 1020). Eighteenth- and nineteenth-century tableware

Fine Art Society, 148 New Bond Street, London W1Y OJT (0171 629 5116). Nineteenth century, artist potters and some contemporary

Gabor Cossa Antiques, 34 Trumpington Street, Cambridge CB2 1QY (01223 356 049). Decorative ceramics, mainly nineteenth century

Valerie Howard, 2 Campden Street, London W8 7EP (0171 792 9702). Quimper, French faience, Mason's Ironstone

Howards of Aberystwyth, PO Box 149, Aberystwyth SY23 1WQ (01545 570 576). Staffordshire figures and animals

Libra Antiques, 131d Kensington Church Street, London W8 7PT (0171 727 2990). Blue-and-white transfer ware and pottery galore

Stephen Long, 348 Fulham Road, London SW10 9UH (0171 352 8226). Highly decorative antique ceramics

Yolanda May, Chelsea Galleries, 69 Portobello Road, London W11 2QB (0181 761 9693). Nineteenth-century teaware

Robert Miller, The Angel, Broad Street, Ludlow, Shropshire (0410 183 683); Decorative ceramics including twentieth-century Wedgwood and Keith Murray

Gillian Neale Antiques, PO Box 247, Aylesbury

HP20 1JZ (01296 423 754). Nineteenth-century British transfer ware

New Century, 69 Kensington Church Street, London W8 4BG (0171 937 2410). Wonderful Dresser, Eltonware and other artist potters, plus some twentieth century

Oliver-Sutton Antiques, 34c Kensington Church Street, London W8 4HA (0171 937 0633). Staffordshire figures and animals

Jacqueline Oosthuizen, 23 Cale Street, London SW3 3QR (0171 352 6071). Staffordshire figures and animals

Rogers de Rin, 76 Royal Hospital Road, London SW3 4HN (0171 352 9007). Wemyss ware, Staffordshire figures and animals

Peter Scott, 5-10 Bartlett Street, Bath BA1 2QZ (01225 466 689). Blue-and-white transfer ware and English pottery

Constance Stobo, 31 Holland Street, London W8 4NA (0171 937 6282). Lustreware, eighteenth- and nineteenth-century pottery

Carolyn Stoddart-Scott (0171 727 5045). Decorative nineteenth-century porcelain and pottery

Target Gallery, 7 Windmill Street, London W1P 1HF (0171 636 6295). Twentieth century, especially post-war and Scandinavian

Tobias and the Angel, 66 White Hart Lane, Barnes, London SW13 OPZ (0181 878 8902). Antique rustic

Robert Young Antiques, 68 Battersea Bridge Road, London SW11 3AG (0171 228 7847). Antique spongeware

### Studio pottery
The following all stock work by contemporary ceramicists:

Barrett Marsden, 17-18 Great Sutton Street, London EC1V 0DN (0171 336 6396).

Contemporary Applied Arts, 2 Percy Street, London W1P 9FA (0171 436 2344).

Crafts Council, 44a Pentonville Road, London N1 9BY (0171 278 7700); and Crafts Council Shop at the Victoria & Albert Museum, London SW7 2RL (0171 589 5070).

Craft Potters Association, 7 Marshall Street, London W1V 1LP (0171 437 7605).

Egg, 36 Kinnerton Street, London SW1X 8ES (0171 235 9315).

Galerie Besson, 15 Royal Arcade, 28 Old Bond Street, London W1X 9FE (0171 491 1706). British and European studio potters

Oxford Gallery, 23 High Street, Oxford OX1 4AH (01865 242 731).

## Modern makers
Altfield, Unit 2/22, Chelsea Harbour Design Centre, Lots Road, London SW10 0XE (0171 351 5893). Chinese-style porcelain of many types

Bridgewater, 739 Fulham Road, London SW6 5UL (0171 371 9033). Modern spongeware

Brixton Pottery, The Forge, Kington, Hereford HR5 3RB (01544 260 644, mail-order). Modern spongeware

Divertimenti, 139-141 Fulham Road, London SW3 6SD (0171 581 8063 or 0171 730 0411 ext 243 for mail order). Provençal and country tableware

Thomas Goode & Co, 19 South Audley Street, London W1Y 6BN (0171 499 2823). Wide selection of classic tableware and bespoke china

Isis repro delftware; modern Lunéville flower patterns; Richard-Ginori designs, for stockists 01865 722 729.

Mrs Monro, 16 Motcomb Street, London SW1X 8LB (0171 235 0326). Anne Gordon's botanical ceramics and decorative ware

Renwick & Clarke, 190 Ebury Street, London SW1W 8UP (0171 730 8913). Clever modern and traditional patterns; decorative and tableware

Wetheriggs Country Pottery, Clifton Dykes, Penrith, Cumbria CA10 2DH (01768 892 733). Traditional slipware

Mary Wondrausch, The Pottery, Brickfields, Compton, Surrey GU3 1HZ (01483 414 097). Slipwares, including commemorative pieces

Zelli, 30a Dover Street, London W1X 3RA (0171 493 0203). Modern Meissen birds and figures and other Continental porcelain

## EUROPE
Diners en Ville, 27 rue de Varenne, 75007 Paris (331 42 22 78 33). Stylish tableware

Dragesco-Cramoisan, 13 rue de Beaune, 75007 Paris (331 42 61 18 20). Eighteenth-century French soft-paste; Vincennes and Sèvres

Kunsthandel Dr Holz, Im Rothsiefen 17, Königswinter, D-53639 Germany (49 22 44 1212). Meissen

Christophe Perles, 20 rue de Beaune, 75007 Paris (33 1 49 26 03 24). Antique French faience

Heinz Reichert, Prannerstrasse 7, Munich 80333, Germany (49 89 22 08 46). Meissen

La Tuile à Loup, 35 rue Daubenton, Paris 75005 (331 47 07 28 90). Traditional country earthenware and leafy plates

## US
Bardith, 901 Madison Avenue, New York, NY 10021 (212 737 3775). Eighteenth- and nineteenth-century porcelain

Garth Clark Gallery, 24 West 57th, Suite 305, New York, NY 10019 (212 246 2205). Contemporary studio ceramics

Helen Drutt Gallery, 1721 Walnut Street, Philadelphia, PA 19103 (215 735 1625). Contemporary studio ceramics

Lynn G. Feld at Bergdorf Goodman, 5th Avenue & 57th Street, New York, NY 10019 (212 753 7300 ext 8398). Eighteenth- and nineteenth-century blue-and-white porcelain, transferware and teaware

Jill Fenichell Inc. Antique Porcelain, 305 East 61st Street, New York, NY 10021 (212 980 9346). Eighteenth- to twentieth-century English and French, plus mail-order catalogue and bespoke

Linda Horne Antiques, 1015 Madison Avenue, New York, NY 10021 (212 772 1122). Majolica and nineteenth-century European porcelain

The Ivy House, 5500 Greenville Avenue, Suite 806, Old Town, Dallas, Texas, TX 75206 (214 369 2411). Wedgwood

Leo Kaplan Ltd, 967 Madison Avenue, New York, NY 10021 (212 249 6766). Eighteenth century

Frank Lloyd Gallery, 2525 Michigan Avenue – B5B, Santa Monica, CA 90404 (310 264 3866). Contemporary studio ceramics

The Meissen Shop, 329 Worth Avenue, no 5, Palm Beach, Florida, FL 33480 (561 832 2504).

Perimeter Gallery, 210 West Superior Street, Chicago, IL 60610 (312 266 9473). Contemporary studio ceramics

James Robinson, 480 Park Avenue, New York, NY 10022 (212 752 6166). Eighteenth and

nineteenth-century English and Continental

Earle D. Vanderkar of Knightsbridge, 305 East 61st Street, New York, NY 10021 (212 308 2022). Eighteenth-century porcelain and pottery

Maria & Peter Warren Antiques Inc., 340 Pequot Avenue, PO Box 686, Southport, Connecticut, CT 06490 (203 259 7069). Mainly creamware

Dorothy Weiss, 256 Sutter Street, San Francisco, California, CA 94108. (415 397 3611). Contemporary studio ceramics

## AUCTION HOUSES
### UK
**Bearnes**, St Edmunds Court, Okehampton Street, Exeter EX4 1DU (01803 296 277 and 01392 207 000). Ceramics sales once a month
**Bonhams**, Montpelier Galleries, Montpelier Street, London SW7 1HH (0171 393 3900). British studio pottery a specialty
**Christie's**, 8 King Street, St James's, London SW1Y 6QT (0171 839 9060); **Christie's South Kensington**, 85 Old Brompton Road, London SW7 3LD (0171 581 7611). General and specialist nineteenth- and twentieth-century ceramics sales
**Dreweatt Neate**, Donnington Priory, Newbury, RG14 2JE (01635 31234). Regular ceramics sales
**Phillips**, 101 New Bond Street, London W1Y 0AS (0171 629 6602). Regular ceramics sales
**Sotheby's**, 34–35 New Bond Street, London W1A 2AA (0171 493 8080). Ceramics sales

### US
**Butterfield and Butterfield**, 220 San Bruno Avenue, San Francisco, CA 94103 (415 861 7500)
**Christie's**, 502 Park Avenue, New York, NY 10022 (212 546 1000); **Christie's East**, 219 East 67th Street, New York, NY 10021 (212 606 0400); **Christie's Los Angeles** (310 385 2600)
**Sotheby's**, 1334 York Avenue, New York, NY 10021 (001 212 606 7000)

## UK MARKETS
**Alfie's Antiques Market**, 13-25 Church Street, London NW8 8DT (0171 723 6066). Factory finery and twentieth-century delights
**Bath Antiques Market**, Guinea Lane, off The Paragon (01225 337 638). Wednesday mornings
**Bermondsey Antiques Market**, 158 Bermondsey Street, London SE1 3TQ (0171 378 1000). Every Friday morning
**Camden Passage**, London N1 8ED. Antique shops plus a Wednesday and Saturday market
**Grays Antique Market**, 58 Davies Street, London W1Y 2LP (0171 629 7034). Islamic, oriental and majolica
**Portobello Road Antiques Market**, Portobello Road, London W11. Friday mornings and Saturdays

# where to see

ceramics collections in museums and houses open to the public

## UK
### London
**British Museum**, Great Russell Street, London WC1 3DG. Wide-ranging collection
**Fenton House**, Windmill Hill, London NW3 6RT (National Trust). Eighteenth-century European and English porcelain; oriental
**Kensington Palace**, London W8 4PX. Late seventeenth- and eighteenth-century Chinese and Japanese porcelain in grand displays
**Linley Sanbourne House**, 18 Stafford Terrace, Kensington, London W8 7BH. Nineteenth-century family collection in the original setting
**Percival David Foundation of Chinese Art**, 53 Gordon Square, London WC1H 0PD. Tenth-to eighteenth-century Chinese ceramics
**Wallace Collection**, Manchester Square, London W1M 6BN. Tip-top Sèvres porcelain
**Victoria & Albert Museum**, Cromwell Road, London SW7 2RL. Superb collection of c. 70,000 pieces encompassing most types

### Outside London
**Ashmolean Museum**, Beaumont Street, Oxford OX1 2PH. Good general collection
**Bowes Museum**, Barnard Castle, Co Durham DL12 8NP. Wonderful collection of European porcelain; lovely coffee cups
**Brighton Museum and Art Gallery**, Church Street, Brighton BN1 1UE. English 1700-1900 plus European Art Nouveau and Art Deco
**Burghley House**, Stamford, Lincolnshire PE9 3JY. Seventeenth- and eighteenth-century Japanese and Chinese, English and Continental
**Castle Museum**, Norwich NR1 3JU. Lowestoft porcelain, Twining teapot collection
**Clandon Park**, West Clandon, near Guildford, Surrey GU4 7RQ (National Trust). The Gubbay collection of Chinese Export birds, English and Continental porcelain
**Clevedon Court**, Tickenham Road, Clevedon BS21 6QU (National Trust). Eltonware
**Conwy Teapot Museum**, at Paul Gibbs Antiques, 25 Castle Street, Gwynedd L32 8AY
**Derby Museum & Art Gallery**, The Strand, Derby DE1 1BS. Derby repository
**Dyrham Park**, Chippenham SN14 8ER (National Trust). Blue-and-white delftware
**Dyson Perrins Museum**, Southern Street, Worcester WR1 2NE. Good Worcester
**Fitzwilliam Museum**, Trumpington Street, Cambridge CB2 1RB. Good general collection
**Hampton Court Palace**, Surrey KT8 9AU. Late seventeenth and early eighteenth century Chinese and Japanese export porcelain
**Hauteville House**, St Peter Port, Guernsey: Victor Hugo lived and decorated here 1856-70
**Holburne Museum**, Great Pulteney Street, Bath BA2 4DB. Antique and contemporary ceramics and a craft study centre

**Hove Museum and Art Gallery**, Church Road, Hove, East Sussex BN3 4AB. English porcelain and contemporary ceramics
**Knole**, Sevenoaks, Kent TN15 0RP (National Trust). Betty Germain's eighteenth-century china closet; also Sèvres and Worcester
**Manchester City Art Galleries**, Lloyd Street, Manchester M60 2LA. Wide-ranging collection including early Meissen and De Morgan
**Minton Museum**, London Road, Stoke-on-Trent, ST4 7QD. Minton
**Mompesson House**, The Close, Salisbury, Wiltshire SP1 2EL (National Trust). Bessemer Bequest. Eighteenth-century porcelain
**Polesden Lacey**, Great Bookham, near Dorking, Surrey RH5 6BD (National Trust). Eighteenth- and nineteenth-century porcelain
**The Potteries Museum and Art Gallery**, Bethesda Street, Hanley, Stoke-on-Trent ST1 3DW. Excellent Staffordshire wares
**Royal Museum of Scotland**, Chambers Street, Edinburgh EH1 1JF. Broad collection of oriental, European and British ceramics
**Shugborough**, Milford, near Stafford ST17 0XB (National Trust). Rare eighteenth-century Chinese porcelain
**Spode**, Church Street, Stoke-on-Trent ST4 1BX. Factory, shop and museum of Spode
**Upton House**, near Banbury OX15 6HT (National Trust). Eighteenth-century French and English soft-paste porcelain
**Waddesdon Manor**, near Aylesbury, Buckinghamshire HP18 0JH (National Trust). Fabulous Sèvres and Chinese porcelain
**Wallington**, Cambo, Morpeth, Northumberland NE61 4AR (National Trust). Eighteenth-century English porcelain, including rare Bow figures
**Wedgwood Museum**, Barlaston, Stoke-on-Trent ST12 9ES. Small museum and temporary exhibitions

## Denmark
**Frederiksberg Castle**, Copenhagen. Porcelain-decked room
**Royal Scandinavia**, Frederiksberg, Copenhagen. Factory and museum; Chinese, Meissen, Sèvres and Royal Copenhagen

## France
**Maison de Victor Hugo**, Paris. Displays of china designed by the writer himself
**Musée de la Céramique**, Rouen. Sixteenth- to nineteenth-century faience
**Musée de l'hôtel Sandelin**, Saint-Omer. Exceptional faience
**Musée des Arts Décoratifs**, Palais de Louvre, Paris. Excellent ceramics
**Musée des Faïence du Vieux Forge**, Forges-les-Eaux. Earthenware
**Musée National Adrien Dubouché**, Limoges. French porcelain and faience

**Musée National de Céramique**, Sèvres. Much Sèvres, European faience and Iznik

## Germany
**Bayerisches Nationalmuseum**, Munich. Includes Bavarian ceramics
**Kunstgewerbemuseum**, Berlin. Sixteenth to twentieth century; good Art Deco
**Museum für Kunst und Gewerbe**, Hamburg. A broad range, Art Nouveau of note
**Schloss Charlottenburg**, Berlin. Wonderful Chinese Porcelain Room, plus Berlin porcelain collection
**Zwinger Palace Museum**, Dresden. Fabulous oriental and Meissen porcelain

## Italy
**Museo Internazionale delle Ceramiche**, Faenza. Exceptional Etruscan, Egyptian and modern (some Picasso vases)
**Palazzo Reale di Capodimonte**, Naples. Italian porcelain

## The Netherlands
**De Porceleyne Fles**, Delft. Delftware factory
**Keramiekmuseum**, Het Princessehof, Leeuwarden. Varied collection
**Museum Mesdag**, The Hague. Porcelain from the Oud Rozenburg factory
**Rijksmuseum**, Amsterdam. Blue-and-white and Meissen porcelain

## Spain
**El Buen Retiro**, Madrid. A similar porcelain cabinet to that in the **Palacio Real**, Madrid.
**Museo de Artes Decorativas**, Madrid. Hispano-Moresque pieces

## Sweden
**Hallwylska Museum**, Norrmalm. Eclectic private collection of Countess von Hallwyl
**National Art Museum**, Stockholm. Excellent Scandinavian ceramics including Art Nouveau
**Röhsska Museum**, Gothenburg. From early dynasty Chinese to modern ceramics
**Skansen Open-air Museum**, Stockholm. Blue-and-white and stoneware

## US & Canada
**Nelson Atkins Museum of Art**, Kansas City, Missouri. Burnap Collection of English pottery; excellent Asian and European porcelain
**Buten Museum of Wedgwood**, Merion, Pennsylvania. Fine Wedgwood
**The Art Institute of Chicago**. African ceramics and European decorative arts from 1100 to the present, some in replica period rooms
**The Colonial Williamsburg Foundation**, Virginia. Eighteenth-century English
**Cooper-Hewitt Museum**, New York. From

# index

Ancient Greek to contemporary ceramics worldwide

**Cummer Museum of Art**, Jacksonville, Florida. Superb Meissen

**Detroit Institute of Arts**. Broad range

**Everson Museum of Art**, Syracuse, New York. Over 5,000 pieces, of which 3,500 are American

**Freer Gallery of Art**, Washington, DC. A distinguished Asian collection art plus James McNeill Whistler's Peacock Room

**Frick Collection**, New York. Stunning Sèvres, Chinese blue-and-white

**George R. Gardiner Museum of Ceramic Art**, Toronto, Ontario. Including Pre-Columbian, European porcelain and modern pottery

**J. Paul Getty Museum**, Santa Monica, California. From sixteenth-century Medici to major eighteenth-century factories, especially Vincennes and Sèvres

**International Museum of Ceramic Art at Alfred**, New York. Studio pottery

**Los Angeles County Museum of Art**. A broad range of Pre-Columbian, medieval, Renaissance, eighteenth-century European and contemporary ceramics

**Metropolitan Museum of Art**, New York. First-rate wide-ranging collection

**Mint Museum**, Charlotte, North Carolina. Wide collection; outstanding plates

**Museum of Fine Arts**, Boston. A comprehensive collection; Asian ceramics and European andEnglish porcelain

**Philadelphia Museum of Art**. Important Sèvres collection, also Italian maiolica, porcelain, stoneware and American ceramics

**Henry Francis DuPont Winterthur Museum**, Delaware. Early English and American pottery.

# acknowledgements

My thanks to the following for their help, advice, kindness and generosity:
Gary Atkins; Andrew Barrow; Nadine Bazar; Laura Church; John Clark; Anthony Collett; Amicia de Moubray; Richard Dennis; June Ducas; Christina Freyberg; Ivry Freyberg; Valerian Freyberg; Mary-Jane Gibson; Nell Graville; Angelo Hornak; Jonathan Horne; Roderick Jellicoe; Claire Johnsen; Tim Knox; Mary Lee-Steere; Stephen Long; Harry Lyons; Smith and Michael O'Connor; Hugh Montgomery-Massingberd; James Mortimer; Pierre Perrone; Ian Price; David Queensberry; Peter Rose and Albert Gallichan; Adrian Sassoon; Mary Scott; Dasha Shenkman; Christopher Simon Sykes; Peyton Skipwith; Carolyn Stoddart-Scott; Target Gallery; Mike Tighe; Sue Timney; Paul Tippett; Susan Walter; Ray Watkins; Mary Wondrausch; Ed Wolf; Andrew Wood